First U.S. paperback edition, April 1965

Reprinted, August 1978

ISBN 0-8028-1120-5

PHOTOLITHOPRINTED BY EERDMANS PRINTING COMPANY
GRAND RAPIDS, MICHIGAN, UNITED STATES OF AMERICA

THE
CHRISTIAN FAITH
IN THE
MODERN WORLD

by

J. GRESHAM MACHEN, D.D., Litt.D.

WM. B. EERDMANS PUBLISHING CO.

Grand Rapids   Michigan

THE CHRISTIAN FAITH IN THE
MODERN WORLD

PREFACE

DURING the first four months of the year 1935, the writer of this book delivered over Station WIP a course of radio addresses, for which the arrangements were made by the Rev. Edwin H. Rian, on behalf of Westminster Theological Seminary, Philadelphia. The addresses are now published in a form very similar to that in which they were delivered. The resulting book may perhaps lay claim to a larger degree of unity than that which is usually possessed by published addresses, since these addresses proceeded in logical sequence. Little more than a beginning, however, is made of the treatment of the subject indicated in the title. The Christian view of the Bible and a part, at least, of the Biblical doctrine of God are presented (of course only in summary fashion); but other great elements in the Christian Faith—the Christian view of man and the Christian view of salvation—are left for future treatment.

The author desires to express his heartfelt gratitude to his friend, the Rev. Edwin H. Rian, of the Board of Trustees of Westminster Theological Seminary, to whom the plan for the delivery of such a course of lectures was due, and whose unfailing encouragement and help made possible the carrying out of the plan. The author is also indebted to colleagues in the Faculty of the Seminary—particularly to Mr. John Murray, who is in charge of the Department of Systematic Theology—for counsel generously given him with regard to certain of the subjects treated in the lectures.

CONTENTS

THE CHRISTIAN FAITH IN THE
MODERN WORLD

I

THE PRESENT EMERGENCY
AND HOW TO MEET IT

At the very beginning, I may as well tell you plainly that I am not going to talk about the topics that are usually regarded as most timely just now. I am not going to talk to you about the gold standard or about unemployment or about the NRA or about the Brain Trust. Possibly some of you may discover that certain things that I may say have a bearing upon those topics, but those topics are not the topics about which I am going to talk.

Instead, I am going to talk to you about God, and about an unseen world.

May I reasonably expect you to be interested in such very intangible topics as these?

There are many persons who say, "No." We are living, say these persons, in the midst of a serious emergency. One economic system, they say, seems to have broken down, and another is not quite ready to be put into its place. Everywhere are to be found unemployment and distress, almost everywhere there are wars or rumors of wars. In the midst of such distresses, who, these persons say, could be so heartless as to spend his efforts upon doubtful speculations regarding a life beyond the grave? Time enough to deal with that other world when we have set this world in order! Let us deal bravely—so the argument runs—first with the problems that we can see; and then, when we have done that, we may possibly find opportunity afterwards to deal with the unseen and intangible things.

I have much sympathy with persons who speak in that way. I do not mean that I agree with them. On the contrary I disagree with them with all my soul. But I do say that I can sympathize with them, and I think I can recognize the element of truth in what they say.

It is certainly true that circumstances do alter a man's choice of the things to which he shall turn his attention. If you were living at Little America along with Byrd, I could hardly advise you to go in to any great extent for landscape-gardening. What is true, moreover, of different positions on the earth's surface is true also of different times. There *are* times of emergency when work that is needed in ordinary times is no longer in place.

The World War, of course, gave us a stock example. In time of war people turned their attention to things very different from the things that they did at ordinary times. If I may use the very humblest of all examples, the example of myself, I may say that in the time of peace before the war I taught Greek; in time of war I made what I am afraid was the world's worst effort at running a small delicatessen store. Other persons did things that were more useful but were even more remote from their ordinary occupations. It was a time of emergency, and things that were ordinarily needed were no longer in place.

I am perfectly ready to admit, moreover, that although the World War is now over the emergency remains with us to the full. Indeed, the emergency is far more serious than we could ever have imagined it would be. Little did I think, for example, as I walked out through the little town of Synghem on the Scheldt River in Belgium on the morning of November 11, 1918, and saw the dead lying beside the road and went out into the positions across the river so recently occupied by the enemy, and as I gloried in the strange peace of that November morning when the noise of war that had so long seemed to be an inevitable part of human existence gave place to a strange, eloquent, unbelievable silence—little did I think, and little did men far wiser than I think, that the peace then vouchsafed to humanity would result after sixteen years in a condition like that which faces us today. Little did I think that a war supposed to make the world safe for democracy would be followed by an era in which in Italy and in Germany, as well as in Russia, democracy and liberty would be openly despised and would be replaced by a tyranny far more crushing and soul-killing in many respects than the cruder tyrannies of the past. Little did I think that even in America the civil and religious liberty which was our dearest possession and which was won by our fathers at such cost would be threatened as it is being threatened today.

No thoughtful man can possibly look out upon the world today without observing that we are in the midst of a tremendous emergency. It does seem perfectly clear to thoughtful people, whether they are Christians or not, that humanity is standing over an abyss.

At such a time, is it any wonder that this world with its pressing problems should seem to many persons quite sufficient to occupy all our thoughts; is it any wonder that the pressing problems that are before our very eyes should crowd out attention to God and to an unseen world?

Persons who adopt that attitude may with some plausibility argue that the most important thing that you have to do for a man is not always the first thing that you must do for him. If a man is in the water, drowning, the most important thing to do for him is to preach the gospel to him for the saving of his soul. But that is not the first thing to do for him. The first thing to do for him is to pull him out of the water. He cannot even attend to the gospel for the saving of his soul when his ears are full of salt water. The first thing that you have to do for him—even though it be not the most important thing—is to pull him out of the water and give him artificial respiration. Then and then only can you preach the gospel to him for the saving of his soul.

It might seem to be the same way with humanity as a whole. Humanity is drowning in the water, or, to change the figure slightly, is sinking in the mire. The first thing to do might seem to be to pull it out, in order that after it has been pulled out we may ask it to deal with the unseen things. Let the Church show what it can do with the plain emergency as it actually exists in this world—so the argument might run—and then, if it proves able to do that, the world may think it worth listening to if it talks about God.

Plausible reasoning this is—plausible but utterly untrue.

In the first place, the program that this reasoning proposes will not work. It proposes that we shall first deal with the political and social emergency, and then afterwards deal with the unseen things. But what was it that brought the emergency upon us in the first place? Was it something in the realm of that which can be seen? Not at all. The physical resources of the world were amply sufficient for the world's needs. No, the thing that brought the emergency upon us was something in the realm of the unseen things. It was an evil that was found within the soul of man.

That evil was not quite so simple as was at first supposed. Not many of us, I think, would now hold that the war was due solely to the sins of the Kaiser or the German military machine. The evil, alas, was considerably more widespread than that. But at least it is clear that it lay within the realm of those intangible and unseen things. It lay within the soul of man and within the sphere of the relations between man and the unseen world.

Moreover, if it was something within that realm that brought the emergency to us in the first place, it is also something in that realm that keeps the emergency with us today. The distress of the world is due clearly to an evil that is within the soul of man.

Hence these so-called "practical" men who would neglect the realm of the soul and of the soul's relations to God in order to deal with the economic problems of the day are the most impractical people that could possibly be imagined. They always remind me of a man who tries to run a gasoline engine that is not producing a spark. You may have your engine in fine working order; there may be a good flow of gasoline; there may be the most perfect lubrication: but if there is something wrong with the ignition system your engine will not run. I think I remember trying the experiment inadvertently sometimes in those heroic days before the invention of self-starters when a Ford was still a Ford. I cranked my engine until I was very red in the face and until my temper suffered considerable strain. I imagined that I needed an expert capable of discoursing on the most intricate principles of dynamics. But despite all my efforts and despite all my search for mechanical learning the miserable engine would not start. Why? Because there was anything wrong with the engine? Not at all. Henry Ford had done his work well. But because I had forgotten to turn on the switch. So it is with these practical men who are not interested in the human soul and in God. They are cranking the engine of society furiously; they are proposing all sorts of radical changes in the machinery. But there is one little thing that they have forgotten. They have forgotten to turn on the switch. The engine is not producing a spark; and until it produces a spark it will not run.

The truth is that that analogy of the drowning man does not apply to the evils of society. To pull a drowning man out of the water is a simple physical effort. But to pull society out of the mire into which it has fallen today is not a simple physical effort at all, but is a highly complex matter; and at the very heart of it is that mysterious portion of the mechanism which is known as the soul of man.

It is impossible, therefore, to deal first with the social and political evils of the day, and then deal afterwards with the unseen things, for the simple reason that without dealing with the unseen things you cannot deal successfully with those social and political problems at all.

At that point I am particularly anxious to avoid mis-understanding of what I am saying. I certainly do not mean by what I have been saying that religion is to be regarded merely as a means to a higher end. I certainly do not mean that God is to be dragged in merely to help us out in the troubles that face us at the present emergency. If I meant that I should be rejecting the central things of the Christian religion and should be saying something quite contrary to the Bible.

We ought to be perfectly clear about this point. If you regard religion merely as a means to attain worldly ends, even the highest and noblest of worldly ends—if you regard religion for example, merely as a means of meeting the present emergency in this world, then you have never even begun to have even the slightest inkling of what the Christian religion means. God, as He is known to the Christian, is never content to be thus a mere instrument in the hands of those who care nothing about Him. The relation to God is the all-im-portant thing. It is not a mere means to an end. Every-thing else is secondary to it.

But what I do mean is that God has so ordered the course of this world that in this case—unlike that case of the drowning man—it is impossible to attain the lower end until the higher end has been attained. It is impossible to deal successfully even with these political and social problems until we have come to be right with God. No emergency can possibly be so pressing as to permit us to postpone attention to the unseen things.

Indeed, the emergency ought to have exactly the opposite effect; the evils of the time, instead of leading us away from God, ought to lead us to Him. There was a time not so very long ago when this world might have seemed to a superficial observer to be a fairly satisfactory place. Even then the evil was there, but it was covered up; the abyss over which we were standing was concealed by the amenities of modern life. When I was a student in Germany in the years 1905-1906, the world might have seemed to a superficial observer to be getting along fairly well without God. It was a fine, comfortable world, that godless European world before 1914. And as for another European war, that seemed to be about as far beyond the bounds of possibility as that the knights should don their armor and set their lances again in rest. The international bankers, we supposed, obviously would prevent an anachronism so absurd. But we have since discovered our mistake. That godless European and American world proved to be not so comfortable after all.

Today the world is in a state far more disquieting than that which prevailed in 1918. Europe is armed to the teeth. Russia stands under the most systematic and soul-crushing tyranny that the world has ever seen. In Germany fiendish wickedness is being practised in the name of science, and in that country as well as in Italy even the form of liberty, to say nothing of the reality of it, has been abandoned. Civil and religious liberty is being treated openly as though it had been merely a passing phase in human life, well enough in its day, but now out of date. In America, the same tendencies are mightily at work. Everywhere there rises before our eyes the spectre of a society where security, if it is attained at all, will be attained at the expense of freedom, where the security that is attained will be the security of fed beasts in a stable, and where all the high aspirations of humanity will have been crushed by an all-powerful State.

Is this a time when we ought to be contented with things as they are? Is it not rather a time when we ought seriously to ask ourselves whether there is not some lost secret which must be regained if humanity is to be saved from the abyss?

What is true about humanity as a whole is also true, I venture to think, about you. The world is weary and perplexed today. Well, how is it with you? Are you contented with your lives as they are now? I suppose that many of you are. But some of you, I know, are discontented, and are looking for something entirely different from that which you now possess. That is true of rich as well as of poor; it has little to do with your particular situation in this world. To such hungry souls I think I have something to say in this little series of talks; and there are many hungry souls today.

But why is it that I have something to say to you? Is it because I am an expert in religion and because I can draw upon great resources of wisdom and experience in order to help you to deal with the problems of your lives? Is it because I am a skillful soul-physician who can point you to hidden resources in your own souls upon which you yourselves can then draw? I may as well say at once that if that is the program of these addresses I cannot expect you to attend to them any more. There are many persons in the world, there are many persons speaking "over the air," who are far wiser and more learned and in every way more gifted than I. No, I certainly cannot expect you to listen to me because of any wisdom of mine; for I have none. I cannot expect you to be particularly interested in any opinions of mine that I may be bold enough to present.

There is just one reason why I may possibly expect you to listen to me. I may expect you to listen to me if I can bring to you a message from God. If I can do that, then the very insignificance of the speaker may in a certain sense be an added inducement to you to listen to him, since it may help you to forget the speaker and attend only to the message.

It is just that that I am trying to do. I am asking you to turn away from me and my opinions; I am asking you to turn away from yourself and your opinions and your troubles; and I am asking you to turn instead that you may listen to a word from God.

Where can I find that word? I am going to try to tell you in the next one of these little talks. Not in myself and not in you, but in an old Book that has been sealed by the seals of prejudice and unbelief but that will, if it is rediscovered, again set the world aflame and that will show you, be you wise or unwise, rich or poor, the way by which you can come into communion with the living God.[1]

[1] The subject of this first talk has been treated by the author in a way which in part is similar in his articles, "Christianity and Liberty," in *Forum* for March, 1931, and "The Responsibility of the Church in Our New Age," in *The Annals* of the American Academy of Political and Social Science for January, 1933.

II

HOW MAY GOD BE KNOWN?

In the first talk of this little series, I tried to tell you why I think you cannot postpone attention to God and to an unseen world. It is true that this world presents pressing problems, but you can never solve even those problems aright unless you first face the question of your relation to God. That is the all-important thing, and the distresses of the present time only serve to press it still more insistently upon our attention.

But if it is important for us to face the question of our relation to God, how can God be known to us? How can we discover whether there is a God at all, and then, if there is, what sort of being He is?

I have something rather simple to say about that question at the very start. It is something that seems to me to be rather obvious, and yet it is something that is quite generally ignored. It is simply this—that if we are really to know anything about God it will probably be because God has chosen to tell it to us.

Many persons seem to go on a very different assumption. They seem to think that if they are to know anything about God they must discover God for themselves.

That assumption seems to me to be extremely unlikely. Just supposing for the sake of the argument that there is a being of such a kind as that He may with any propriety be called "God," it does seem antecedently very improbable that weak and limited creatures of a day, such as we are, should discover Him by our own efforts without any will on His part to make Himself known to us. At least, I think we can say that a god who could be discovered in that way would hardly be worth discovering. A mere passive subject of human investigation is certainly not a living God who can satisfy the longing of our souls.

Some years ago I was asked to contribute to a composite volume which had as its general title, "My Idea of God." [1] Various writers told, each of them, what his own idea of God was. One said, "I think of God so"; another said, "I think *so*." Now I shall not presume to say whether the essay that I contributed to that volume had any particular merit at all. Perhaps it was a rather poor effort. But I do very deliberately maintain that I was right at least in saying at the beginning of it that if *my* idea of God were really mine I should attach very little importance to it myself and could reasonably expect even less importance to be attributed to it by others.

A divine being that could be discovered by my efforts, apart from His gracious will to reveal Himself

[1] *My Idea of God*, edited by Joseph Fort Newton, Litt.D., D.H.L., 1926.

to me and to others, would be either a mere name for a certain aspect of man's own nature, a God that we could find within us, or else at best a mere passive thing that would be subject to investigation like the substances that are analyzed in a laboratory.

I think we ought to stick to that principle rather firmly. I think we ought to be rather sure that we cannot know God unless God has been pleased to reveal Himself to us.

How, then, has God revealed Himself to us?

In the first place, He has revealed Himself by the universe that He has made. How did the world come into being? It is here. That cannot be denied. But how did it come to be?

The question forces itself upon the attention of every thinking man. We may try to evade it. We may just say that it is unanswerable. We may try to put it out of our minds. But it continues to haunt us all the same, and for ages it has haunted the human race.

I think the universe itself provides the answer to that question. The answer is itself a mystery, but it is a mystery in which we can rest. The answer is a very simple answer. The answer is that the world came into being because God made it. It is the work of an infinite and all-wise and all-powerful God.

That answer presses itself upon different people in different ways. It has been defended by philosophers and theologians by way of detailed reasoning. That reasoning has been divided logically into what are called the "theistic proofs"—indications in the world itself that point to the existence of a personal God, creator and ruler of the world.

I am not going to speak of them here except just to say that I think they are good proofs, and that the Christian man, whether he has a detailed knowledge of them or not, ought never to depreciate them or regard as a matter of no importance the debate about them among philosophers and learned men.

But I am not going to attempt any exposition of those proofs. What I do want to do is just to point out that the testimony of nature to nature's God comes to different people in different ways. I remember listening some time ago to a lecture by an eminent man of science. The lecturer traced the progress of scientific investigation and pointed out, if I remember aright, its material benefits. But then he paused to speak of another product of the scientific spirit; the true scientist, he said, is brought face to face at last with the ultimate mystery, and at that point he becomes a religious man. There is endless diversity in the world, said he: but the progress of investigation has revealed the electron; and the electrons, said he, are all alike—they are machine-made—and their marvellous likeness reveals the existence of a mystery into which man cannot penetrate; in truly religious awe the man of science stands at length before a curtain that is never lifted, a mystery that rebukes all pride.

I am not saying that man of science had a true knowledge of God. I do not think that he had. I should have liked, if he had been willing to listen to me, to tell him of the way in which, for little children as well as for learned men of science, that dreadful curtain of which he spoke has been pulled gently aside to give us at least a look into the mysteries beyond. But at least there was one aspect of nature that brought that scientist to the threshold of a knowledge of God.

To some men the testimony of nature to nature's God comes by such precise knowledge of nature as was possessed by that scientist. To others it comes by a reasoned consideration of the implications of nature's existence. But to still others it comes by what Browning calls "a sunset touch." To one man in one way, to another in another.

To me nature speaks clearest in the majesty and beauty of the hills. One day in the summer of 1932 I stood on the summit of the Matterhorn in the Alps. Some people can stand there and see very little. Depreciating the Matterhorn is a recognized part of modern books on mountain-climbing. The great mountain, it is said, has been sadly spoiled. Why, you can even see sardine-cans on those rocks that so tempted the ambition of climbers in Whymper's day. Well, I can only say that when I stood on the Matterhorn I do not remember seeing a single can. Perhaps that was partly because of the unusual masses of fresh snow which were then on the mountain; but I think it was also due to the fact that unlike some people I had eyes for something else. I saw the vastness of the Italian plain, which was like a symbol of infinity. I saw the snows of distant mountains. I saw the sweet green valleys far, far below, at my feet. I saw the whole glorious round of glittering peaks, bathed in an unearthly light. And as I see that glorious vision again before me now, I am thankful from the bottom of my heart that from my Mother's knee I have known to whom all that glory is due.

Then I love the softer beauties of nature also. I wonder whether you love them with me. Some years ago, in the White Mountains, I walked beside a brook. I have seen, I suppose hundreds of brooks. But somehow I remember particularly that one. I am not going to tell you where it is, because if I did you might write to the C.C.C. or the National Park Service about it and get them to put a scenic highway along it, and then it would be forever ruined. But when I walked along it, it was untouched. I cherish the memory of it. It was gentle and sweet and lovely beyond all words. I think a man might travel through all the world and never see anything lovelier than a White Mountain brook. Very wonderful is the variety of nature in her changing moods.

Silence too, the silence of nature, can be a very revealing thing. I remember one day when I spent a peaceful half-hour in the sunlight on the summit of a mountain in the Franconia range. I there experienced something very rare. Would you believe it, my friends? It was really *silent* on that sunny mountain top. There was not the honk of a motor horn; there was no jazz music; there was no sound of a human voice; there was not even the rustling of the leaves. There was nothing but a strange, brooding silence. It was a precious time indeed. I shall never forget it all my life.

Please do not misunderstand me. I am not asking that everyone should love the beauties of nature as I love them. I do think, indeed, that the love of nature ought to be cultivated. At least I do not think that government ought to go into the business of crushing it out of a people's soul as the United States government is doing by some of the artificialities and regularities of its National Parks. I think some sweet and delicate little things ought to be left untouched. But I well understand that there are many people who do not love the beauties of nature. Are they shut off from finding God revealed in the world that He has made?

Indeed, that is not so, my friends; indeed, it is not so. The mystery of the existence of the world presses itself upon different people in different ways. I remember, for example, a talk that I heard from a professor at an afternoon conference service many years ago. I do not know just why I should remember it, but I do remember it. The professor said that he had had a friend who had come to a belief in God, or had come back to a belief in God, by—what do you suppose? Well, by a trip through Europe! As he went from city to city and observed the seething multitudes, the throngs upon throngs of men and women, somehow, he said, the conviction just seemed to come over him: "There is a God, there is a God."

Was that a foolish fancy? Were those experiences in my own life of which I have been bold enough to speak merely meaningless dreams? Or were they true testimonies to something marvellous beyond? Were they moments when God was graciously revealing Himself to me through the glory of the world that He has made?

I think a Christian ought not to be afraid to give the latter answer. The revelation of God through nature has the stamp of approval put upon it by the Bible. The Bible clearly teaches that nature reveals the glory of God.

In a wonderful passage in the first chapter of the Epistle to the Romans the Apostle Paul says that "the invisible things of him from the creation of the world are clearly seen, being understood by the things that are made, even his eternal power and Godhead." Here the Bible approves the arguments of those who in systematic fashion argue from the existence of the world to the existence of a divine Maker of the world. But the Bible also approves those more unreasoned flashes of knowledge in which suddenly we see God's work-manship in the beauty and the majesty of His world. "The heavens declare the glory of God; and the firma-ment sheweth his handywork," says the Psalmist. And what said our Lord Jesus Christ. "Even Solomon in all his glory," said He of the lilies of the field, "was not arrayed like one of these."

All that is true. The revelation of God through na-ture is a very precious thing. But then a serious ques-tion arises. If God has revealed Himself through the things that He has made, why do so very few men listen to the revelation? The plain fact is that very few men arrive by a contemplation of nature at a true belief in a personal God. Even those scientists whose religious views are sometimes being incautiously welcomed by Christian people are often found upon closer examina-tion to believe only in a God who is identical with a spiritual purpose supposed to inhere in the world proc-ess itself and are found not to believe at all in a living and holy God, are found not to believe at all in the true God who created the heavens and the earth.

Why is that so? If God has revealed Himself so plainly through the world that He has made, why do men not see?

Well, when men do not see something, there are two possible explanations of the fact. One is that there is nothing there to see. The other is that the men who do not see are blind.

It is this latter explanation which the Bible gives of the failure of men to know God through the things that He has made. The Bible puts it very plainly in that same passage already quoted from the first chapter of Romans. "Their foolish heart," says Paul, "was darkened." Hence they did not see. The fault did not lie in nature. Men were "without excuse," Paul says, when they did not see what nature had to show. Their minds were blinded by sin. That is a hard saying, but like many other hard sayings it is true. You will never understand anything else that I may say unless you understand that we all of us, so long as we stand in our own right, and have not had our eyes mysteriously opened, are lost and blind in sin.

III

HAS GOD SPOKEN?

AT the beginning of this little series of talks, I tried to tell you why you cannot postpone attention to an unseen world and to God. This world presents very pressing problems just now, but even the problems of this world cannot be solved aright if you neglect the other world and the great question of your relation to God. Then I began to tell you how you can come into relations with that unseen world; I tried to begin to tell you how God may be known. He may be known, I said, through the universe that He has made: the existence of the world shows that there is a Maker and Ruler of the world.

That revelation of God through nature, I said, is wonderfully confirmed by the Bible, but it does not come only from the Bible. It is spread out before men so that all might be expected to see.

But in the last of these talks I was not able to finish, even in bare outline, what ought to be said about that general revelation of God which is given to us outside of the Bible. I spoke of the way in which God has spoken to us through the majesty and beauty of the world that He has made. But there is another way, still apart from the Bible, in which God has spoken to His creatures. He has spoken not only in the wonders of the world outside of us but also through His voice within. He has planted His laws in our hearts. He speaks to all men through the voice of conscience. He speaks through the majestic words which all but the most degraded men utter, the words: "I ought." He speaks through the majesty of the moral law. A law implies a lawgiver. Conscience testifies of God.

There are some people, even people who are not Christians, to whom that revelation seems particularly to appeal. Some years ago I remember hearing an informal lecture by a well-known professor of philosophy. The speaker told us about the present state of philosophical opinion. It was, he said, overwhelmingly in favor of naturalism—that is, very few philosophers believed in any reality beyond and above the universe in which we live. He himself, the speaker said, disagreed with this naturalism. He did believe in a transcendent reality. Why? He believed in it, he said, because he observed that certain people sacrifice their own interests for the sake of other people or for the sake of duty. What could possibly lead them to act so if there is no transcendent principle of right? How could they possibly act in a way so contrary to all worldly interests unless there is a reality beyond this world?

The Bible sets the stamp of its approval upon that

revelation of God through conscience, as we have seen that it sets the stamp of its approval upon the revelation that comes through the external world. Paul says, for example, in the second chapter of the Epistle to the Romans: "For when the Gentiles, which have not the law, do by nature the things contained in the law, these, having not the law, are a law unto themselves: which shew the work of the law written in their hearts, their conscience also bearing witness, and their thoughts the mean while accusing or else excusing one another. . . ." [1] Here the Apostle does seem clearly to teach that the voice of conscience, which speaks in the very constitution of man's nature, is the voice of God. He does not mean that men really obey that law as it ought to be obeyed. On the contrary, he is very clear indeed in teaching that all have disobeyed. They have disobeyed the law, but at least the law is there, in their hearts. Because of their disobedience they are under the condemnation of the law; the law can therefore of itself never give them any hope. But that is not the fault of the law; the moral law is written in the very constitution of their being, and if they do not heed it they are without excuse.

Thus God the great lawgiver is revealed in the voice of conscience as He is in the wonders of the world without. These two may be grouped together as constituting the revelation of God through nature, if nature

[1] Rom. 2:14 f.

be taken to include the nature of man. The philosopher Immanuel Kant is said to have summed it up when he spoke of the starry heavens above and the moral law within as being the two things which fill the heart of man with awe. I do not mean that those two things gave to Immanuel Kant a true knowledge of God: I do not mean even that he had a true notion of what knowledge itself is. But what I mean is that he made a correct summary of those things which apart from the Bible ought to give us a knowledge of God. The wonders of the universe without and the moral law within —those are the two great elements in God's revelation of Himself through nature.

But He has not only revealed Himself through nature; He has also revealed Himself in an entirely different way. That other revelation of God, different from His revelation of Himself through nature, is not natural but supernatural.

When we say "supernatural," we are not speaking about something contrary to nature. Nothing that is contrary to nature could possibly come from God; for God is the author of nature, and He cannot contradict Himself.

But when we say that anything is "supernatural" we are saying that it is "above nature."

There is a really existing order of nature; the order of nature does not consist merely in our observation of certain regularities in God's working, but it is something that truly exists.

That does not mean that nature exists apart from God. On the contrary, it would not continue to exist for one moment except by God's will. God is not isolated from the world; He does everything that nature does and He says everything that nature says.

But what we mean is that God acts and speaks in two very different ways. In the first place He acts and speaks by means of the world that He has made; and in the second place He acts and speaks directly, without the use of means.

It was in this latter way that God acted when He first created the world, and it was in this latter way that He acted when He wrought the miracles recorded in the Bible and when He spoke to men in the supernatural revelation with which we are dealing just now.

Why was this supernatural revelation needed?

It was needed for two reasons.

In the first place, God's revelation of Himself through nature has been hidden from our eyes by sin. We saw in the last talk how that is the case with the revelation given by the wonders of the external world. Those wonders reveal the glory of God. But men are blinded so that they do not see. That is even more clearly true of the revelation of God through His voice within. Have you never experienced yourselves, my friends, the way in which conscience becomes blunted? Have you never first looked upon some foul thing with horror, and then slipped into that thing by insensible **degrees,** so that what **seemed** wrong to you before is now treated as a matter of course, until at some sad hour you come to yourself and see that you are already wallowing in the mire? Ah yes, the voice of conscience is silenced by a life of sin. We can detect that dreadful hardening process in ourselves, and very terribly is it set forth in the Bible as a punishment for sin. How terrible, too, are the perversions of the conscience among men! It is certainly true that the revelation of God through conscience has been hidden from men's eyes by sin.

There is need of supernatural revelation, therefore, to show us again those things which sin has hidden from our eyes.

But is that all the supernatural revelation that there is? If it were, we should be of all men most miserable. Suppose we had had revealed to us the terrible majesty of God; suppose the voice of conscience had spoken to us with perfect clearness, of the justice of God and of our disobedience. How terrible that revelation would be!

No, thank God. He has also, in His supernatural revelation, told us other things. He has told us again in supernatural fashion things that we ought to have learned through nature, but then He has told us other things of which nature gives no slightest hint. He has told us, namely, of His grace. He has told us of the way in which sinners who have offended against His holy law and deserve nothing but His wrath have been made His children at infinite cost and will live as His children for evermore.

Where shall we find that supernatural revelation? I want to say very plainly that I think all that we can know of it now is found in the pages of one Book.

There have, indeed, been men in our day who have claimed to be the recipients of supernatural revelation, who have claimed to be prophets, who have said as they have come forward: "Thus saith the Lord; God has spoken directly to me, and my voice therefore is the voice of God."

But those who have said that in our times are false prophets one and all; the real supernatural revelation that we know is recorded in one blessed book, the Bible.

It is no wonder that that is the case, because there is a marvelous symmetry and completeness in that revelation of God which the Bible records. I should love to speak to you about it if there were time. When sin came into the world, the Bible tells us that there was a revelation of salvation to come; the seed of the woman should bruise the serpent's head. I should love to tell you of the unfolding of that promise. I should love to tell you of Abraham and of Moses. I should particularly love to tell you of the great prophets, because in their words we see so plainly what supernatural revelation is. They spoke of judgment; they spoke of the terror and the majesty of God. But they also spoke, very tenderly, of God's grace. As when at some solemn sunset hour there are dark clouds above but low on the horizon a deep, clear, unearthly light, despair of every artist's brush, so in the great prophets there are warnings of the day of vengeance of our God but mingled with the warnings strange gleams of a heavenly tenderness and peace. "For unto us a child is born, unto us a son is given: and the government shall be upon his shoulder: and his name shall be called Wonderful, Counsellor, The mighty God, The everlasting Father, The Prince of Peace." "Behold, a virgin shall conceive, and bear a son, and shall call his name Immanuel."

Only, our figure was not altogether right; those passages reveal to us not a sunset glow but the glory of a far-off dawn. Then, as we read the Bible, we see the dawn drawing nearer. It is like that solemn hour when all nature is hushed before the appearance of the day. Shepherds kept watch over their flocks by night. There came to them a heavenly word: "Unto you is born this day in the city of David a Saviour, which is Christ the Lord." I should love to tell you of that Saviour. He spake as never man spake. But I suppose His whole life can be called supernatural revelation. He was true man, but He was not only man, and He came into this world by a supernatural act of God, and in His death and resurrection He wrought a supernatural work. I should love to tell you of the way in which through the apostles supernatural revelation was gloriously continued after His saving work was done. I should love to tell you how by heeding the revelation contained in the Epistles of the New Testament you can have that glorious Saviour as your Saviour today. I should love to tell you of the last book of the Bible, with its promises of things to come, with its promises of the time when we shall see our Saviour face to face.

Yes, there is a wonderful symmetry and completeness in the supernatural revelation recorded in the Bible.

But one question may trouble us. Have we a true *record* of that revelation? The revelation came to men of long ago. How do we know that the account which we have of it is true? And how do we know that those saving acts of God which went with the revelation really did happen? The revelation is one thing, it might be said, and the record of the revelation is another. How do we know that the record is true?

I want to talk to you about that question in the next one of these addresses. I want to talk to you about inspiration—the inspiration of the Book in which the revelation is recorded. I want to talk to you about the question just exactly what we mean when we say that the Bible is the Word of God.

IV

IS THE BIBLE THE WORD OF GOD?

IN the last two talks in this series, I have been speaking to you about the question how God may be known. He may be known, I said, only as He has been pleased to reveal Himself But He has been pleased to reveal Himself in two ways In the first place, He has been pleased to reveal Himself through nature—by the wonders of the world and by His voice within, the voice of conscience—and, in the second place, He has been pleased to reveal Himself in an entirely different way that we call supernatural" because it is "above nature" We were talking about that supernatural revelation in the last talk In that supernatural revelation God has spoken to men not through the wonders of the world that He has made and not through His voice planted in our hearts, the voice of conscience, but directly and specially, in a way analogous to the way in which one person here on earth gives a piece of information to another

I said at the close of the little talk that all of that "supernatural" or special revelation that we know is contained within the pages of one book, the Bible. Was I right in saying that?

Well, I think that I was just about right. Supernatural revelation, along with the miracles, ceased when the last of the Apostles of Jesus died. If you want information as to why the miracles ceased, and with them supernatural revelation, I think you will find it if you will turn, for example, to the admirable book by the late B. B. Warfield, entitled "Counterfeit Miracles." [1]

But why should we not obtain information, in addition to that recorded in the Bible, about supernatural revelation given, indeed, not later, but in Bible times? Well, it is perfectly conceivable that we might do so. It is perfectly conceivable, for example, that there might turn up in Egypt bits of papyrus affording true information about words of Jesus not contained in the four Gospels. But the bits of papyrus which have actually turned up so far hardly seem to provide such information. It is, for example, on the whole unlikely that Jesus really spoke the words recorded in one such fragment: "Lift up the stone, and there thou shalt find me; cleave the wood, and there I am." [2] On the whole, speaking broadly, we can certainly say that all the supernatural revelation that we can be at all certain about, although no doubt other supernatural revelation was given in Bible times, is recorded in the pages of one book, the Bible.

But then the question forces itself upon our atten-

---

[1] Warfield, *Counterfeit Miracles,* 1918, pp. 1-33.
[2] For text and translation, see Hugh G. Evelyn White, *The Sayings of Jesus from Oxyrhynchus,* 1920, pp. 35 f.

tion 'How about *that* record?" We have said that the record of supernatural revelation outside the Bible is uncertain, to say the very best for it. But is the record *in* the Bible any better? Can we really depend upon the record?

I want to try to answer that question today. I want to try to tell you what I think the right view of the Bible is.

In doing so, I am perfectly well aware of the fact that in the opinion of a good many people I shall be putting my worst foot forward. I shall be giving expression to views which put me out of accord with the main trend of opinion both outside the Church and inside of it. Should I not be wiser if I took this thing more gradually, if I adopted a more apologetic line of approach, if I decided, in the first part of my little series at least, to conceal somewhat the full unpopularity of my opinions?

In reply, I just want to say that I do not think that if I adopted that method I should be treating you quite fairly. Here we are, sitting down together quietly. Cannot we at least be friends? Cannot we at least try to understand each other, whether we can agree with each other or not? I do not think that I should be doing my part toward that mutual understanding if I concealed from you the real basis of what I am going to say.

Hence I am going to tell you at once, just as briefly

and as plainly as I can, what I think about the inspiration of the Bible.

As I do that I am afraid I shall have to relinquish any ambitions of being brilliant or sparkling or eloquent. A simple, summary presentation of a large subject does not lend itself to the exercise of these qualities. So I must resist the temptation of exhibiting my eloquence. That is just too bad! But I do not think I can estimate my self-sacrifice in this particular too highly. You see, I am greatly assisted in my battle against the temptation of exhibiting my eloquence by the fact that I have no eloquence to exhibit.

At any rate, whether because of necessity or because of choice, I am subordinating all other ambitions in these little talks to the one ambition of being plain. I do want to try to help you to get certain things straight. They may seem to be simple and even elementary, and yet there is the strangest confusion about them today. You may not agree with me about these things, but at least I hope that if you are broadminded enough to listen to me at all you may obtain a fairer conception about what certain much abused people—we who believe in the inspiration of the Bible—really hold. After all, there are a good many people in the world who believe, as I do, that the Bible is the Word of God; and you cannot really be broadminded, you cannot really have an intelligent view of the state of humanity as a whole, if you listen only to what is said about these people by their opponents and never take the trouble to listen to what they have to say for themselves.

Of course, I cannot conceal from you the fact that I have also another and a higher purpose in these little talks. I want not only to clear away misconceptions from your minds as to what we believe, but I want to win some of you to believe the same thing yourselves. I want not only to show you what are the views of people who believe that there is a God and that He has spoken to men, but also to try to lead some of you to listen to the voice of God for yourselves. I know I cannot do that by any mere persuasions or arguments of mine. I can do it only if I have the blessing of God. But if I can just be the instrument, in these little talks, to clear away the mists and to enable you to see God, above all if I can bring you a message from God's Word as to how you can come into God's presence and become His child—if I can do that even for a single one of you— then these little talks will have been well worth while.

What, then, shall we think about the Bible? I will tell you very plainly what I think we ought to think I will tell you very plainly what I think about it I hold that the Biblical writers, after having been prepared for their task by the providential ordering of their entire lives, received, in addition to all that, a blessed and wonderful and supernatural guidance and impulsion by the Spirit of God, so that they were preserved from the errors that appear in other books and thus the resulting book, the Bible, is in all its parts the very Word of God, completely true in what it says regarding matters of fact and completely authoritative in its commands.

That is the doctrine of full or "plenary" inspiration of Holy Scripture. It is not a popular doctrine. It is not in accordance with the wisdom of this world. A man cannot hold to it seriously (and really act in accordance with it) and at the same time enjoy the favor of the world or the favor of the ecclesiastical authorities in many of the churches of the present day. Yet it is a very blessed doctrine all the same, and if a man founds his life upon it he can be very joyous and quite undismayed in all the sorrows and all the battles that may come upon him in this world.

Now I want to talk to you a little about that blessed doctrine of the inspiration of the Bible. It is certainly worth talking about, because it belongs not to the superstructure but to the foundation. If a man really holds to it, everything else for that man is changed.

But can a man hold to it? Is it a reasonable thing to believe in the plenary inspiration of the Bible? And if it is a reasonable thing, how can we show that it is a reasonable thing? I cannot attempt to answer that latter question with any fulness in the rest of the present little talk. But I do believe that some of the objections to the doctrine of the plenary inspiration of the Bible disappear the minute a man observes clearly what that doctrine is, and in particular the minute he observes what that doctrine is not. The strangest misconceptions prevail, even among people who otherwise are educated people, about what we believers in the plenary inspiration of the Bible really hold. Perhaps I can perform a service by clearing away one or two of those misconceptions now.

In the first place, then, let it be said that we believers in the plenary inspiration of the Bible do not hold that the Authorized Version or any other form of the English Bible is inspired. I beg your pardon for saying anything so obvious as that, but, do you know, my friends, it is necessary to say it. There are scarcely any limits to the ignorance which is attributed to us today by people who have never given themselves the trouble to discover what our view really is. Let it be said then very plainly that we do not hold that the Authorized Version or any other form of the English Bible is inspired. We are really quite well aware of the fact that the Bible was written in Hebrew and in Greek. The Authorized Version is a translation from the Hebrew and the Greek. It is a marvelously good translation, but it is not a perfect translation. There are errors in it. The translators were not supernaturally preserved from making mistakes. It is not inspired.

In the second place, we do not hold that any one of the hundreds, even thousands, of the Greek and the Hebrew manuscripts of the Bible is free from error. Before the invention of printing the Bible was handed down from generation to generation by means of copies made by hand. Those copies were written out laboriously by scribes. Before one copy was worn out or lost another copy would be made to take its place, and so the Bible was handed down. Hundreds of thousands, perhaps—no one knows how many—of such copies or "manuscripts" were made. Several thousand of them, some of these containing of course only parts of the Bible or only parts of either Testament, are now in existence. These are just remnants from among the vast number that are lost. Now we believers in the inspiration of the Bible do not believe that the scribe who made any one of these manuscripts that we have was inspired. Every one of the manuscripts contains errors; no one of them is perfect. What we do believe is that the *writers* of the Biblical books, as distinguished from scribes who later copied the books, were inspired. Only the autographs of the Biblical books, in other words—the books as they came from the pen of the sacred writers, and not any one of the copies of those autographs which we now possess—were produced with that supernatural impulsion and guidance of the Holy Spirit which we call inspiration.

At that point an objection to the doctrine of inspiration arises in the minds of many people. I am inclined to think it is a widespread objection, and I am inclined to think it troubles many thoughtful and intelligent people. "What is the use of the inspiration of the

Bible," people say, "if no form of the Bible that we now have is inspired? Why should God have worked a stupendous miracle in order to preserve the writers of the Biblical books from error and make the autographs of their books completely true if He intended then to leave the books thus produced to the mere chance of transmission from generation to generation by very human and often careless copyists?"

Such is the objection. I have deep sympathy with the people who raise it or who are troubled by it. It is such a very human objection. We are all of us so prone to say· "If God did this, why did He not also do that?" We are all of us so apt to demand of God just a little bit more than He has given us. We are all of us so reluctant to say to ourselves that perhaps God's way is best, and that in not giving us all He has given us just exactly what it was good for us to have.

But, human though such reasoning is, it is very wrong. What we ought to do as a matter of fact is to take with thankfulness what God has been pleased to give us and not say that because He has not been pleased to give us something else therefore what He has been pleased to give us is of no use.

Certainly in this case with which we are dealing now what He has been pleased to give us is a very great deal, and it is far more than some people seem to think. He has given us the supernatural inspiration of the writers of the Biblical books That is much. But, according to our view of the Bible, that is not all that He has given us. He has also, according to our view, given us a marvelously accurate, though not a supernaturally accurate, transmission, from generation to generation, of what those inspired writers wrote.

The objector says to me, "How strange, according to your view, the view of you believers in the plenary inspiration of the Bible, it is that God should leave the transmission of a supernaturally inspired book to the chance of transmission by fallible human copyists!" What do I say in reply? I say: Hold on there, brother; what is that you said? Did you say that according to our view God left the transmission of the Bible to chance? If you said that you said something that is quite wrong. That is not our view at all. No, God certainly did not, according to our view, leave the transmission of the Bible to chance. He did not leave anything to chance; but it is particularly plain that He did not leave *that* to chance. Was it by chance that in the early days the text of the New Testament books was so diligently copied from one piece of papyrus to another that knowledge of what the sacred writers had written was not lost during the period when that very perishable writing material was used? Was it by chance that about the beginning of the fourth century the wonderfully durable writing material, vellum, or parchment, came into use, so that two great manuscripts of the Bible made in that century are for the most part just as clear and easy to read today as if they had been made yesterday? Was it by chance that one of these manuscripts, the great Codex Sinaiticus, was so strangely preserved in the monastery of St. Catherine on Mount Sinai until it was found by Tischendorf in 1859? Was it by chance that a perfect photographic reproduction of that manuscript has been made, so that although the manuscript itself was well worth the half-million dollars that the British Museum is said to be paying the Soviet government for it, you can obtain to all intents and purposes just as much information about the manuscript as if you had the manuscript itself in your hands, any time you will just come to the library of Westminster Seminary, for example, and look at the photographic reproduction? Is it by chance that the evidence for the original text of the Bible is so vastly more abundant than for the text of other ancient books in the case of which, nevertheless, nobody doubts but that we have a very close approximation indeed to what the authors wrote? Was it by chance that the King James or Authorized Version of the English Bible was made in the most glorious period of the English language and by men so wonderfully qualified for their task?

No, my friends, these things did not come by chance God did these things. He did not do them by a miracle But it was just as much God that did them as it would have been if He had done them by a miracle He did them by His use of the world that He had made and by

His ordering of the lives of His creatures. Very wonderfully and very graciously, according to our view of the Bible, has God provided for the preservation, from generation to generation, of His holy Word.

What is the result for you, my friends? The result is that you can take down your Authorized Version from the shelf, the version hallowed, for many of you, by many precious associations, and be very sure that it will give you good information about that which stood in the autographs of the Word of God. The study of the manuscripts of the Bible is a wonderfully reassuring thing. The Greek text of the New Testament, for example, from which the Authorized Version is taken is based not upon the best manuscripts but upon inferior manuscripts. Yet how infinitesimal is the difference between those inferior manuscripts and the best manuscripts—how infinitesimal in comparison with what they have in common! I do not mean that we ought not to take care in the use of the Bible; I do not mean that we ought not to try by every means within our power to determine what the exact wording of the autographs was. I do think that careful Christian scholarship is a very important thing. Yet God has provided very wonderfully for the plain man who is not a scholar. You do not have to depend for the assurance of your salvation and the ordering of your Christian lives upon passages where either the original wording or the meaning is doubtful. God has provided very wonderfully for the transmission of the text and for the translation into English The Bible is perfectly plain in the things that are necessary for your souls God will make other things in it clearer to you as the years go by Read it, my friends It is God's Book, not man's book It is a message from the King. Read it, study it, trust it, live by it. Other books will deceive you, but not this book. This book is the Word of God.

Many things have been left unsaid this afternoon. Many things are left at loose ends. I do not like to leave things at loose ends when I am talking about the Bible. This theme is so momentous that I always wish when I talk about it that I could say everything at once I am so afraid of leading somebody astray by telling just a part of the truth. So I do hope you will listen to me in the next one of these talks I want to say certain things that simply must be said I want to say something more about what the inspiration of the Bible means. Does it mean a mechanical treatment of the Biblical writers as so many people say it does? In what sense is it, and in what sense is it not, "verbal" inspiration? I want to talk to you about that question. I also want to talk to you about the question whether it is enough to say that the Bible contains a record of supernatural revelation or whether we ought rather to say that it is as a whole itself a supernatural revelation from God.

V

DO WE BELIEVE IN VERBAL INSPIRATION?

IN the last talk I was speaking about the inspiration of the Bible. The writers of the Biblical books, I said, received a blessed and wonderful and supernatural guidance and impulsion by the Spirit of God, so that they were preserved from the errors that appear in other books and thus the resulting book, the Bible, is in all its parts the very Word of God, completely true in what it says regarding matters of fact and completely authoritative in its commands. That is the great doctrine of the full or "plenary" inspiration of Holy Scripture.

I had to break off what I was saying to you about that doctrine. In fact, almost all that I had time to do was to clear away certain misconceptions. Now we get more into the heart of the subject.

I think I can help you to get into the heart of the subject if I just ask you to consider with me for a minute or two what I suppose is one of the commonest if not the very commonest of the objections to the doctrine of full or "plenary" inspiration. You see, this business of considering objections is a good thing in more ways than one. Not only may it possibly help people who are actually troubled by the objections, but also it may enable all of us to get the thing more nearly straight in our minds. There are few better ways of seeing clearly what a thing is than the way of setting it off sharply in contrast with what it is not.

Well, what is this common objection to the doctrine of plenary inspiration? It is that the doctrine of plenary inspiration represents God as acting upon the Biblical writers in a mechanical way, a way that degrades those writers to the position of mere machines.

People who raise this objection sometimes ask us: "Do you believe in the 'verbal' inspiration of the Bible?" When they ask us that, they think that they have us in a dreadful hole. If we say: "No, we do not believe in verbal inspiration," they say: "How then can you hold to your conviction that the Bible is altogether true? If God did not exercise some supernatural control over the words, then the words will surely contain those errors which are found in all human productions." If, on the other hand, we say: "Yes, we do believe in verbal inspiration"—then they hold up their hands in horror. "How dreadful, how mechanical!", they say. "If God really provided in supernatural fashion that the words should be thus and so, then the writers of the Biblical books are degraded to the position of mere stenographers; indeed, they are degraded even lower than that, since stenographers are human enough to err and also to help, whereas in this case the words would be produced with such perfect accuracy as to show that the human instruments in the production of the words were mere machines. What becomes of the marvelous beauty and variety of the Bible when the writers of it are regarded as having been treated in this degrading way?"

Such is the hole into which we are thought to be put; or, if I may change the figure rather violently, such are the horns of the dilemma upon which we are thought to be impaled.

How can we possibly escape? Well, I think we can escape very easily indeed. You ask me whether I believe in the verbal inspiration of the Bible. I will answer that question very plainly and quickly. Yes, I believe in the verbal inspiration of the Bible; but I do insist that you and I shall get a right notion of what the word "verbal" means.

I certainly believe in the verbal inspiration of the Bible. I quite agree with you when you say that unless God provided in supernatural fashion that the words of the Bible should be free from error we should have to give up our conception of the Bible as being, throughout, a supernatural book.

Yes, inspiration certainly has to do with the words of the Bible; in that sense I certainly do believe in verbal inspiration. But if you mean by "verbal inspira-·tion" the view that inspiration has to do *only* with the words of the Bible and not also with the souls of the

Biblical writers, then I want to tell you that I do not
believe in verbal inspiration in that sense. If you mean
by verbal inspiration the view that God moved the
hands of the Biblical writers over the page in the way
in which hands are said to be moved over a ouija board
—in such a way that the writers did not know what they
were doing when they wrote—then I do hold that that
kind of verbal inspiration does utterly fail to do justice
to what appears in the Bible very plainly from Genesis
to Revelation.

The writers of the Bible did know what they were
doing when they wrote. I do not believe that they always knew all that they were doing. I believe that
there are mysterious words of prophecy in the Prophets
and the Psalms, for example, which had a far richer
and more glorious fulfilment than the inspired writers
knew when they wrote. Yet even in the case of those
mysterious words I do not think that the sacred writers
were mere automata. They did not know the full
meaning of what they wrote, but they did know part
of the meaning, and the full meaning was in no contradiction with the partial meaning but was its glorious
unfolding.

I believe that the Biblical writers used ordinary
sources of information; they consulted documents, they
engaged in research, they listened to eyewitnesses.

I do not, indeed, believe, that they were limited to
such sources of information. They were sometimes, as

they wrote, the recipients of fresh supernatural revelation—supernatural revelation not previously given to others but given for the first time to them in the very moment of their writing. I believe also that sometimes even when they used ordinary sources of information or when they consulted their memory their use of such means of information went far beyond what is possible, except with supernatural assistance, to the human mind.

In one sense, of course, their use of such sources of information always went beyond what is possible to the human mind. To err is human, and these men did not err. They were always protected, in supernatural fashion, from the errors which appear in ordinary books.

But what I mean is that sometimes that supernatural heightening of human powers consisted not only in the invariable prevention of error in matters where uninspired writers might in any individual case have avoided error, but also in the prevention of error in matters where uninspired writers could not possibly have avoided error.

I am thinking, for example, of the discourses of Jesus reported in the Gospel according to John. It is often urged as an objection against the authenticity of those long discourses that no one who heard the discourses could possibly have remembered them so long afterwards with anything like accuracy. That objection no longer troubles me as much as it formerly did. Did not our Lord Himself tell the Apostles, including the writer of this Gospel, that after His departure the Holy Spirit would bring to their remembrance whatsoever He had said unto them? [1] May we not suppose that the report by the Beloved Disciple, writer of this Gospel, of the things that Jesus had said when He was with the disciples on earth goes far beyond what is possible to the unaided human memory and is due in part to that mysterious and supernatural work of the Holy Spirit of which Jesus spoke?

But such considerations ought not to obscure the fact that the Biblical writers did use ordinary sources of information where they were reporting things that had been said and done on this earth. Indeed, they often lay great stress on the fact that they used such ordinary sources of information. The author of that very Gospel about which we have just been speaking, and in which we were inclined to find something that goes far beyond what is possible to the unaided human memory—even the author of that Gospel lays particular emphasis on the fact that he was an eyewitness of the life of Jesus. He reported what he had seen and heard. He did not tell these things just because they had been revealed to him at some later time in some supernatural experience. No. He was there when Jesus said certain things and did certain things. As an eyewitness he in-

[1] John 14:26.

sists that he is worthy of belief. Even before his hearers or his readers should come to believe in any supernatural inspiration of which he was the recipient they ought to believe him as men believe a credible witness when he takes his seat on the witness-stand.

So the Apostle Paul appeals to the witness of the five hundred brethren who had seen the risen Lord. So the Evangelist Luke tells in the prologue of his Gospel about the historical researches in which he had been engaged. Yes, the Biblical writers used ordinary sources of information, and when they were eyewitnesses they used their own memory of what they had seen and heard.

It is very important indeed to insist upon these facts, because they give the Bible such evidential force. Suppose a man comes to the reading of the Bible without any belief in inspiration. Even then he ought to give credence to what he reads. It can be shown him even before any acceptance on his part of the doctrine of plenary inspiration that the writers were men who had opportunities of knowing the facts, that they were honest men, that they knew how to distinguish truth from falsehood. If he will only consider these Biblical books with the same fairness as that with which he approaches other sources of historical information, he will accept what they say as being substantially true. Then, on the basis of that conviction that they are substantially true, he will go on to see that the books are not only substantially true, in the way in which other good books are true, but that they are altogether true because of the supernatural work of the Spirit of God.

We do not therefore merely *admit* that the Biblical writers used ordinary sources of historical information. We *insist* upon it. It is tremendously important for the witness which the Bible renders to those who have not yet come to believe.

What is more, the Biblical writers did not merely use ordinary means of obtaining information, but also they followed their own individual habits of style. When people say that the doctrine of plenary or full inspiration of the Bible fails to do justice to the individuality of the Biblical writers, they simply show that they do not know what they are talking about. Yes, what a wonderful variety there is in the Bible. There is the rough simplicity of Mark, the unconscious, yet splendid eloquence of Paul, the conscious literary art of the author of the Epistle to the Hebrews, the matchless beauty of the Old Testament narratives, the high poetry of the Prophets and the Psalms. How much we should lose, to be sure, if the Bible were written all in one style!

We believers in the full inspiration of the Bible do not merely admit that. We *insist* upon it. The doctrine of plenary inspiration does not hold that all parts of the Bible are alike; it does not hold that they are all equally beautiful or even equally valuable; but it only holds that all parts of the Bible are equally true, and that each part has its place.

That wonderful variety in the Bible did not come by chance. It came by the gracious providence of God. It was God who superintended the varied education of those writers to prepare them the better for their mighty task. It was God who watched over the prophet Amos when he was "an herdman and a gatherer of sycomore fruit." It was God who watched over Paul when he sat at the feet of Gamaliel. When I consider the wonderful variety among the Biblical writers, and the wonderful unity of the Book amid this variety, I am tempted to use a figure of speech to describe what is really beyond all human figures. I am tempted to think of the writers of these sixty-six books as though they were a great orchestra, not composed of poor mechanical strummers but of true musicians, carefully chosen, carefully trained, individual, different, yet contributing by their very differences to the unity of some glorious symphony under a great Director's wand. In that marvelous harmony of Holy Scripture even the least considered parts of the Bible have their place. None could be lacking without offending the great Musician's ear.

But, you say, this doctrine of inspiration is certainly a great paradox. It holds that these men were free, and yet that every word that they wrote was absolutely determined by the Spirit of God. How is that possible?

How could God determine the very words that these men wrote and yet not deal with them as mere machines?

Well, my friend, I will tell you how. I will tell you how God could do that. He could do it simply because God is God. There is a delicacy of discrimination in God's dealing with His creatures that far surpasses all human analogies. When God deals with men He does not deal with them as with machines or as with sticks or stones. He deals with them as with men.

But what needs to be emphasized above all is that when God dealt thus with the Biblical writers, though He dealt with them as with men and not as with machines, yet He accomplished His ends. He ordered their lives to fit them for their tasks. But then, in addition to that providential ordering of their lives, in addition to that use of their individual gifts of which we have spoken, there was a supernatural work of the Spirit of God that made the resulting book not man's book but God's Book.

That supernatural work of the Spirit of God extends to all parts of the Bible. People say that the Bible is a book of religion and not a book of science, and that where it deals with scientific matters it is not to be trusted. When they say that, if they really know what they are saying, they are saying just about the most destructive thing that could possibly be imagined.

Is religion really independent of science? Well,

"religion" is a very broad term. I will not say just how broad a term it is. Possibly it is even broad enough to include an attitude of the human soul that is independent of all facts with which science may legitimately deal. I am not saying whether such an attitude may or may not be called "religion." I am not much interested in the question. What I am interested in and what I am certain about is that whatever may be true of religion in general, the *Christian* religion is most emphatically dependent upon facts—facts in the external world, facts with which "science" in the true sense of the word certainly has a right to deal.

When you say that the Bible is a true guide in religion, but that you do not care whether it is a true guide when it deals with history or with science, I should just like to ask you one question. What do you think of the Bible when it tells you that the body of the Lord Jesus came out of that tomb on the first Easter morning nineteen hundred years ago? That event of the resurrection, if it really happened, is an event in the external world. Account would have to be taken of it in any ideally complete scientific description of the physical universe. It is certainly a matter with which science, in principle, must deal. Well, then, is that one of those scientific matters to which the inspiration of the Bible does not extend, one of those scientific matters with regard to which it makes no difference to the devout reader of the Bible whether the Bible is true or false?

There are many people who say just that. There are many people who do not shrink from that logical consequence of their division between religion and science. There are many people who say that the Bible would retain its full religious value even if scientific history should show that it is wrong about the resurrection of Jesus and that as a matter of fact Jesus never rose from the dead.

I say there are many people who say that. But the people who say that are not Christians. We Christians know that we are sinners; and we look to the Bible for something far more than inspiring poetry or soul-stirring exhortation or expert instruction in the art of being religious. We look to the Bible for facts.

What good does it do to me to tell me that the type of religion presented in the Bible is a very fine type of religion and that the thing for me to do is just to start practising that type of religion now? What good does it do to tell me that I have a fine pattern of religion in the account of Jesus in the Gospels whether that account is history or an inspiring ideal? What good does it do to tell me to cultivate my religious nature in the manner in which the religious nature was cultivated with such eminent success by Jesus or by Paul or by Isaiah?

I will tell you, my friend. It does me not one tiniest little bit of good. You are just mocking me when you talk to me like that. You are ignoring my true condition. You are ignoring the fact that in my own right

I am a sinner under the wrath and curse of God, and that in my own strength I am under the awful bondage of sin. What *I* need first of all is not exhortation but a gospel, not directions for saving myself but knowledge of the way God has saved me. Have you any good news for me? That is the question that I ask of you. I know your exhortations will not help me. But if anything has been done to save me, will you not tell me the facts?

The Bible does tell me the facts. It tells me Jesus died on the cross to save me; it tells me He rose from the dead to complete His saving work and be my living Lord. What do I say when it tells me that? Do I say: "That is history and not religion: I am not interested in it; it may be true or it may not be true for all I care; the Bible is a book of religion and not a book of science or a book of history"? No, my friends, I do not say that. I say rather: "Praise be to God for that blessed story of the resurrection and the cross; upon the truth of it all my hope depends for time and for eternity; how I rejoice that God Himself has told me in His holy Book that it is true!"

Here is a rule for you, my friends: no facts, no good news; no good news, no hope. The Bible is quite useless unless it is a record of facts.

Thank God, it is a record of facts. The Spirit of God, in infinite mercy, was with the writers of the Bible not merely when they issued God's commands, but also and just as fully when they wrote the blessed record of what God had done.

What a dreadfully erroneous thing it is to say merely that the Bible *contains* the Word of God. No, it *is* the Word of God. It is the Word of God when it records the facts. It is the Word of God when it tells us what we must do.

Hear it as the Word of God, my friends. It will probe very deep into your life. It will reveal the dark secrets of your sin. But then it will bring you good tidings of salvation as no word of man can do.

VI

SHALL WE DEFEND THE BIBLE?

In the last few talks in this little series, I have been speaking to you about the inspiration of the Bible. I have been saying that the Bible is the Word of God and that as such it is completely true in matters of fact and completely authoritative when it issues commands.

That is certainly a good deal to say; it is certainly a large claim for me to make in behalf of a book that many people regard merely as a collection of Hebrew religious literature.

The question arises whether the claim is justified, whether the Bible is really and truly the Word of God.

I have a great deal of sympathy for those who raise that question, and I do not think that it is a question that ought to be dodged. If you should come into the classes that I try to conduct at Westminster Seminary, I do not believe that you would charge me with dodging the question. I do try as best I can—only, I wish my best were better—to show the students how we can deal with people who do not yet believe in the inspiration of the Bible. We cannot help them very much if we just assume that they already believe what we believe. Instead, we ought to try to understand their present position and then lead them logically from one thing to another until finally we can show them that the Bible is, as we believe it is, the Word of God.

When I say that, I do not mean that everyone who comes to believe in the inspiration of the Bible passes successively through those logical steps. In countless cases conviction as to the divine authority of the Bible comes in very much more immediate fashion. A man hears some true preacher of the gospel. The preacher speaks on the authority of a book which lies open there on the pulpit. As the words of that book are expounded, the man who listens finds that the secrets of his heart are revealed. It is as though a cloak had been pulled away. The man suddenly sees himself as God sees him. He suddenly comes to see that he is a sinner under the just wrath and curse of God. Then from the same strange book there comes a wonderful offer of pardon. It comes with a strange kind of sovereign authority. The preacher, as he expounds the book, seems to be an ambassador of the King, a messenger of the living God. The man who hears needs no further reflection, no further argument. The Holy Spirit has opened the doors of his heart. "That book is the Word of the living God," he says; "God has found me out, I have heard His voice, I am His for ever "

Yes, it is in this way, sometimes, and not by elaborate argument, that a man becomes convinced that the Bible is the Word of God.

Yet that does not mean that argument is unnecessary. Even that man in our illustration may meet criticism of his new-found conviction. People may tell him that the book which he thinks to be the Word of God is really full of errors and absurdities. How is he going to meet such criticism? Well, "that depends." He may be able, because of his intellectual gifts, to meet the criticism squarely; he may be able to meet the critics on their own ground and to show that as a matter of fact the Bible is *not* full of errors and absurdities. Or he may be a simple soul unable to say any more to the critics of his new-found conviction than that which was said by that man in the ninth chapter of John: "One thing I know, that, whereas I was blind, now I see."

But whatever may be possible to that converted man in our illustration, it is perfectly clear, when you take the Christian world as a whole, that convictions are held by but a precarious tenure if those who hold them continue, on principle, to ignore objections. After all, truth is essentially one. I may be convinced with my whole soul that the Bible is the Word of God; but if my neighbor adduces considerations to show that it is really full of error, I cannot be indifferent to those considerations. I can, indeed, say to him: "Your considerations are wrong, and because they are wrong I can with a good conscience hold on to my convictions." Or I can say to him: "What you say is true enough in itself, but it is irrelevant to the question whether the Bible is the Word of God." But I do not see how in the world I can say to him: "Your considerations may be contrary to my conviction that the Bible is the Word of God, but I am not interested in them; go on holding to them if you want to do so, but do please agree with me also in holding that the Bible is the Word of God."

No, I cannot possibly say that This last attitude is surely quite absurd. Two contradictory things cannot both be true. We cannot go on holding to the Bible as the Word of God and at the same time admit the truth of considerations that are contrary to that conviction of ours.

I believe with all my soul, in other words, in the necessity of Christian apologetics, the necessity of a reasoned defence of the Christian Faith, and in particular a reasoned defence of the Christian conviction that the Bible is the Word of God.

Some years ago I attended a conference of Christian students. Various methods of Christian testimony were being discussed, and particularly the question was being discussed whether it is necessary to engage in a reasoned defence of the Christian faith. In the course of the discussion, a gentleman who had had considerable experience in work among students arose and said that according to his experience you never win a man to Christ until you quit arguing with him. Well, do you know, my friends, when he said that I was not impressed one tiny little bit. Of course a man never was won to Christ *merely* by argument. That is perfectly clear. There must be the mysterious work of the Spirit of God in the new birth. Without that, all our arguments are quite useless. But because argument is insufficient, it does not follow that it is unnecessary. What the Holy Spirit does in the new birth is not to make a man a Christian regardless of the evidence, but on the contrary to clear away the mists from his eyes and enable him to attend to the evidence.

So I believe in the reasoned defence of the inspiration of the Bible. Sometimes it is immediately useful in bringing a man to Christ. It is graciously used by the Spirit of God to that end. But its chief use is of a somewhat different kind. Its chief use is in enabling Christian people to answer the legitimate questions, not of vigorous opponents of Christianity, but of people who are seeking the truth and are troubled by the hostile voices that are heard on every hand.

Sometimes, when I have given a lecture in defence of the truth of the Bible, a lecture, for example, which has adduced considerations to show that Christ really did rise from the dead on the third day, somebody has come up to me afterwards and has said very kindly something to the following effect: "We liked your lecture all right, but the trouble is that the people who need it are not here; we who are here are all Christian people, we are all convinced already that the Bible is true, so that we are not the ones who really needed to listen to what you had to say."

When people have told me that I have not been too much discouraged. It is true, I do wish that those persons who do not agree with me might occasionally give me a hearing. It does seem rather surprising that people who pride themselves on being so broadminded should take their information about what is called by its opponents "Fundamentalism" from newspaper clippings or from accounts of "Fundamentalism" written by opponents on the basis of newspaper clippings, instead of reading what these so-called "Fundamentalists," these conservatives, these Christians, have published in serious books over their own signatures, or instead of listening to what they have to say when they lecture. But although I do wish that my opponents in this debate would give me a fairer hearing, yet I am not too much discouraged when they are not present at one of my lectures. You see, what I am trying to do in such a lecture is not so much to win directly people who are opponents of the Bible as to give to Christian parents who may be present or to Christian Sunday-school teachers materials that they can use, not with those whose backs are up against Christianity, but with the children in their own homes or in their Sunday-school classes, the children who love them and want to be Christians as they are Christians, but are troubled by the voices against Christianity that are heard on every side.

Yes, I certainly do believe in Christian apologetics; I certainly do believe in the necessity of the reasoned defence of the truth of the Bible. I have felt it to be my duty to engage in it myself, to the very best of my very limited ability; but what is really important is that many persons far, far abler than I should engage in this great work.

Certainly neglect of this work will be to the loss of countless precious souls. Some years ago a kind of anti-intellectualism prevailed widely in the Church. Scholars were despised by evangelists; theological seminaries were regarded either as nurseries of unbelief or else as places where men engaged in dry-as-dust pursuits remote from living reality.

Well, many theological seminaries today *are* nurseries of unbelief; and because they are nurseries of unbelief the churches that they serve have become unbelieving churches too. As go the theological seminaries, so goes the church. That is certainly true in the long run. Look out upon the condition of the Church throughout the world today, and you will see that it is true.

But why is it that so many theological seminaries have become nurseries of unbelief and have dragged the churches that they serve down with them? It is partly because of that anti-intellectualistic attitude of pastors and evangelists, of which I spoke just now. Despising scholarship as they did, and leaving it in possession of the enemy, they discover today that in the long run they cannot get along without it. When real revival comes in the Church, we may be perfectly sure of one thing. We may be perfectly sure that with it and as a vital part of it will come a revival of Christian learning. That was true of the Reformation of the sixteenth century, and it will be true of every reformation or revival that does any more than merely scratch the surface.

I do wish people would read the twelfth chapter of I Corinthians more often than they seem to do—that chapter where Paul speaks of the diversity of gifts and of that one Spirit who divideth "to every man severally as He will." If they did read that great chapter more carefully, they would see that what was true of the supernatural gifts of the Spirit in the apostolic age is also true of the gifts which the Holy Spirit still graciously bestows upon the Church. It is still quite true that one gift cannot do without the others. Certainly it is true that evangelism cannot do without Christian scholarship. I do not like to think of the relationship between Christian scholarship and evangelism as being a balance between the two things. I do not like to say: "Let us have evangelism, but not so much evangelism as to crowd out Christian scholarship." No, the true state of the case is that you can hardly have evangelism unless you have Christian scholarship; and the more

Christian scholarship you have, so much the more evangelism. Out of real theological seminaries, where the Bible is expounded and defended, come ministers and evangelists who know what they believe and why they believe it; and the preaching of such ministers and evangelists is graciously used of God for the salvation of precious souls. There is no guess-work about that. Look about you today, and you will see that it is simply a fact.

Well, perhaps you may say that I have said enough about the necessity of defending the Bible and ought now to go on and defend it. Obviously I cannot do so today, since my time is nearly up. Also I am not going to be able to do so in any great detail in the following talks of this series, because in this particular series I am going to talk about what the Bible teaches rather than about the reasons which impel us to believe that the Bible is true. At some future time I should particularly love to study the New Testament with you, for example, in order to show you how wonderful are the evidences of its truth, and how wonderfully those evidences of truthfulness confirm our conviction that the whole Bible is indeed the Word of God.

But even now, even in the present talk, I cannot leave you without saying just a word about the way in which we come to that great conviction about the Bible. I want just to indicate very briefly one great argument for the inspiration and divine authority of Holy Scripture. Mind you, it is not the only argument; but I am just singling it out by way of example this afternoon.

That argument is found in the testimony of Jesus Christ. In the first century of our era there lived in Palestine a man called Jesus of Nazareth. We have certain records of His life in the New Testament. I want you to study them at least as historical documents. If you are not yet ready to take them as part of the inspired Word of God, as I do, study them at least, fairly, as historical documents.

If you do study them thus fairly, you will be impressed by the picture which they give of Jesus Christ. That picture is evidently the picture of a real person. Of that there can be no doubt. But it is also the picture of a very strange person. The Jesus of the Gospels advanced stupendous claims and substantiated those claims by a sovereign power over the forces of nature. He seemed to command nature as nature's Maker and nature's God. He was clearly a supernatural person.

Modern men have tried to separate the supernatural from the natural in the Gospel picture of Jesus. "We shall just remove these antiquated supernatural trappings from the picture," they have said to themselves, "and then we shall have a picture of the real Jesus, a great religious genius and nothing more." But the effort to make that separation has been a failure. The supernatural element in the Gospel picture of Jesus has proved to be an integral part of the whole. It cannot be separated from the rest in that easy, artificial way. The Gospel picture of Jesus is supernatural through and through.

Some radicals of the present day are drawing the logical conclusion. Since the supernatural is inseparable from the rest and since they will not accept the supernatural, they are letting the whole go. They are telling us that we cannot know anything at all with any certainty about Jesus.

Such skepticism is preposterous. It will never hold the field. You need not be afraid of it at all, my friends. The picture in the Gospels is too vivid. It is too incapable of having been invented. It is evidently the picture of a real person.

So the age-long bewilderment of unsaved men in the presence of Jesus still goes on. Jesus will not let men go. They will not accept His stupendous claims; they will not accept Him as their Saviour. But He continues to intrigue and baffle them. He refuses to be pushed into their little moulds. They stand bewildered in His presence.

There is only one escape from that bewilderment. It is to accept Jesus after all. Refuse to believe that the picture is true, and all is bewilderment and confusion in your view of the earliest age of the Church; accept the picture as true, and all is plain. Everything then fits into its proper place. The key has been found to solve the mighty riddle.

The supernatural Jesus is thus the key to a right understanding of early Christian history. But He is also the key to far more than that. Mankind stands in the presence of more riddles than the riddle of New Testament times. All about us are riddles—the riddle of our existence, the riddle of the universe, the riddle of our misery and our sin. To all those riddles Jesus, as the New Testament presents Him, provides the key. He is the key not to some things but to everything. Very comprehensive, very wonderfully cumulative, very profound and very compelling is the evidence for the reality of the supernatural Christ.

But if we are convinced by that evidence, we must take the consequences. If we are convinced that Jesus is what the New Testament says He is, then the word of Jesus becomes for us law. We cannot then choose whether we will believe Him when He speaks. We *must* believe. His authority then must for us be decisive in all disputes.

On many questions our records do not record any decision of Jesus. But on one question His decision is plain. It is plain to us not only after we have become convinced that the records of His life are divinely inspired and therefore altogether without error. It is plain even when we take those records merely as reasonably accurate history. If one thing is clear to the historian, it is that Jesus of Nazareth held to the full truthfulness of the Old Testament Scriptures; it is that Jesus held that high view of the divine authority of the Old Testament which is held by despised believers in the Bible today.

That is admitted even by those who have a low opinion of the truthfulness of the Gospels. Jesus, they admit, held that view of the Bible which was held generally by the Jews of His day. They are sorry to admit that. "Too bad," they say, "that Jesus, whom we admire so much, was in this respect a child of His time!" But admit it, if they are scholars, they must. Jesus did certainly believe that the Old Testament was the very Word of God, and He certainly placed that belief at the very heart of His life as a man.

But if He thus pointed back to the Old Testament and founded His human life upon it, He also pointed forward to the New. He chose apostles. He endowed them with a supernatural authority. In exercise of that authority, they gave the New Testament books to the Church. No man who believes what Jesus says can, if he is consistent, help taking the whole Bible as the very Word of God.

When we do take the whole Bible thus as the very Word of God, we find rich and manifold confirmation of our decision. We find it in the marvelous unity of Holy Scripture—what the Westminster Confession calls "the consent of all the parts." We find it in the countless evidences of truthfulness in detail. We find it in the utter dissimilarity of this book to other books. We find it in the sweetness and peace of a life grounded upon what this book tells. Yes, my friends, very rich and varied, yet marvelously convergent, is the evidence that bids us take the Bible as the Word of God.

VII

THE BIBLE VERSUS HUMAN AUTHORITY

IF the Bible is really the Word of God, as we have said it is, the question arises what it actually means in our lives to take the Bible in that way.

I want to talk to you for a little while about that question now.

The answer to the question ought not to be so very difficult, however difficult some of the implications of the answer may turn out to be. If we take the Bible as the Word of God, then the Bible becomes our standard of truth and of life. When we are asked whether we can support any kind of message or can engage in any course of conduct, what we do is simply to compare that message or that course of conduct with the Bible. If it agrees with the Bible, we can support it or follow it; if it does not agree with the Bible, we cannot support it or follow it, no matter what we may be told by other authorities to do.

I really think it is very important that that should be perfectly clear. We are living at a time when a very serious difference of opinion has appeared in the Church. The first question in dealing with any difference of opinion is the question what standard of judgment is to be applied to the question at issue. Unless people can agree about that preliminary question it is not likely that they will agree about anything else.

Suppose I have an engagement with a business man in Philadelphia in the summer time. The engagement is for eleven o'clock. I come in from the country and appear at the office promptly at eleven. But when I get there, I find the man with whom I have the engagement considerably perturbed. "What do you mean," he says, "by keeping me and these other gentlemen waiting in this way? The engagement was for eleven o'clock, and it is now exactly twelve. You are exactly an hour late." I then reply in kind. "You surprise me," I say; "in fact I should really hesitate to characterize the impropriety of your words. My watch says exactly eleven o'clock, and I would back my watch against any cheap office clock in the whole city of Philadelphia." Then, after we have disputed about the matter vigorously for a good while, I discover that Philadelphia is on daylight-saving time. You see, we could not come to any agreement because we were applying different standards to the question under dispute.

It is somewhat that way with the difference of opinion in the Church. There, too, the disputing parties cannot come to an agreement because they are operating with different standards. In one very important particular, however, our illustration of daylight-saving time and standard time does not apply to the situation in the Church. In the case of my imaginary dispute with that business man, both parties to the dispute could be right, because it did not make any particular difference which of the two standards should be applied. It did not make any very great difference whether we should go on daylight-saving time or on standard time, just so we were both of us perfectly clear as to which was being used. But in the case of the situation in the Church both parties to the dispute are laying claim to the same thing—namely, truth. Therefore, they cannot both be right. In this case, the standard that is sought is not just some arbitrary method of dividing up the day, but it is a standard of truth, and truth is not relative but absolute.

However, the illustration does at least show that if two parties to any dispute are to understand each other —to say nothing of coming to an agreement—the first question they must discuss is the question what standard is to be used. Certainly that principle applies in fullest measure to the difference of opinion in the Church. Here we find perfectly earnest and sincere people differing from each other in the sharpest possible way. What one holds to be true the other holds to be false; what one holds to be wise and beneficent the other holds to be destructive. Discussion between the contending parties sometimes seems only to make matters worse; it sometimes seems only to lead to greater irritation and greater confusion. The reason for this unfortunate state of affairs—at least one important reason for it—is perfectly plain. It is found in the fact that the contending parties do not see clearly that the real ground of their difference of opinion is that they have totally different standards of truth and of life.

I have already said what our standard is. It is the Bible. When we are deciding whether we can support any propaganda or engage in any course of conduct, we simply ask whether that propaganda or that course of conduct agrees with the Bible.

I think I can best explain what it means to take the Bible thus as one's standard of truth and of life if I set this standard over against some of the other standards that are being proposed today.

Many persons, for example, are taking human experience as their standard. They are saying that they will adhere to that kind of religion which works the best, which shows itself to be the best in actual practice.

I remember that some years ago I preached a baccalaureate sermon at a college. When I got through, a member of the graduating class asked me what I thought of a certain religious movement, which it is entirely aside from our present point for me to name. I intimated that I could not support it. In reply he told me that he for his part thought it was the most "vital" thing in the religious world today. That young man and I did not get very far in our discussion because we were applying different standards. He was applying the standard of experience; I was applying the standard of the Bible.

That young man favored the religious movement that we were discussing because it was "vital." Well, in one sense noxious weeds in a garden are vital. They often grow up more rapidly than the flowers. But the careful gardener is inclined to pull them up. So also we refuse to make mere rapidity of growth or enthusiasm of adherents the criterion by which any religious movement shall be judged. Instead, we test every movement by the Bible. If it agrees with the Bible, we approve it; if it disagrees with the Bible, we oppose it, no matter what external successes it may attain and no matter even what apparent graces it may seem to our superficial human judgment to induce here and there in its adherents. Those apparent graces, we are sure, will, if the movement is contrary to the Bible, never stand the test to which they will be subjected at the judgment-seat of God. God does not contradict His own Word.

That same use of experience as the standard of truth and of life underlies what I believe has been called somewhere "the great inquiry racket." There has arisen in recent years a perfect craze for questionnaires on the subject of religion, "open forums," and "inquiries" of various kinds. The thing has become one of the major nuisances of the day. When one contemplates the unscientific character of many of these enterprises and their begging of the real underlying questions, one is tempted to dismiss them as being unworthy of consideration. Many of them are not really inquiries at all, but are merely agencies carrying on propaganda through the particular device of question-begging questionnaires. The people who conduct them are of course honest. They are trying to get at the truth: but, the trouble is, they are so completely out of sympathy with the Christian religion that when they formulate their questionnaires they do not know how even to give a Christian man the opportunity of casting his vote or of giving expression to his convictions.

But absurdly unscientific and question-begging though many of these inquiries and questionnaires are, a serious purpose, even though it be a mistaken purpose, does, I think, underlie them. The purpose underlying them is, I think, that through an examination of various types of religion we may arrive, by a process of comparison and elimination, at that type of religion which is best adapted to the age in which we are living and which therefore is the type of religion which it is thought we ought to adopt. Those who engage in these inquiries and questionnaires, or at any rate many of those who engage in them, are making human experience the standard of truth and of life.

That standard is quite different from the standard to which we hold. These persons are advocating a "managed currency" in religion, whereas we are on the gold standard. Our standard is not a flexible standard. Far from holding that what is true today becomes false to-morrow according to the shifting needs of human life, we find our standard both of truth and of conduct in the Bible, which we hold to be not a product of human experience but the Word of God.

So we reject the first alternative view that we are considering in the present little talk. We reject experience as our standard.

In the second place, we reject, as our standard, what is wrongly called "the teaching of Jesus" or "the teaching of Christ." At that point I am particularly anxious not to be misunderstood. I certainly hold that the real teaching of Jesus is all completely true. I hold that everything that Jesus said in the sphere of fact is true and that His commands are all completely valid. But my point is that those who make the teaching of Jesus their authority, *as distinguished from the Bible,* are not really holding to the teaching of Jesus at all. We have seen how clearly Jesus testified to the authority of the Bible. How then, if you reject the authority of the Bible, can you possibly claim to be true to Jesus' teaching?

What is the underlying notion of those who make what they call the teaching of Jesus their authority, instead of the Bible? I am afraid that question is not hard to answer. It is the notion that Jesus was primarily a teacher, that we honor Him because by His word and by His example He taught us how to practise the same type of religion as that which He practised. Jesus, according to this way of thinking, was the founder of Christianity because He was the first Christian. Other men honor Buddha or Confucius as the great teacher and example; we, say the men of this way of thinking, are Christians because we take Jesus, as distinguished from Buddha or Confucius, as *our* teacher and example.

That notion is of course radically contrary to the Bible, but it is also radically contrary to the real Jesus' own teaching. Jesus, according to the Bible and according to His own teaching, came, as has well been observed, not primarily to say something, but to do something. He came not just to teach us true general principles of religion and ethics, but to redeem us from sin by His death upon the cross.

His teaching is indeed very precious. How wonderfully precious it is, my friends! But its preciousness is altogether lost when it is separated from the rest of the Bible. We miss the very heart and core and substance of it if we take it out of its organic connection with that grand sweep of supernatural revelation that runs through the Bible from Genesis to Revelation, and if we separate it from that mighty saving work which culminated in the Cross and resurrection of Christ.

Thus we reject this notion that the teaching of Jesus as distinguished from the Bible is the seat of authority.

It is profoundly dishonoring to the teaching of Jesus itself. It degrades Jesus to the level of a mere religious teacher, the founder of one of the world's religions.

I am inclined to think that most of those who begin by saying that the teaching of Jesus is their authority are, if they reflect about the matter, obliged to modify their position. Jesus obviously said many things which they do not regard as true. But if Jesus said many things that are untrue, how can His teaching be authoritative?

Well, a great many of these men respond, with more or less clearness, that it is not the teaching of Jesus as such—or, as they would put it, not the "letter" of His teaching—but the underlying "spirit" of His teaching which they regard as authoritative.

That brings us to the third of the alternatives to the authority of the Bible which we are now passing under review. It is the alternative of those who say that their authority is "the spirit of Jesus."

Of course when they use the phrase "the spirit of Jesus," they do not mean at all what the Bible means by it. The Bible means by it the Holy Spirit, the Third Person of the blessed Trinity. They, on the other hand, spell the word "spirit" with a small letter, not with a capital, and they mean by "the spirit of Jesus" simply the inner temper or quality of Jesus' life. We are Christians, according to the advocates of this view, not because of any particular thing that Jesus did nineteen hundred years ago, not even because we obey any particular commands that He uttered, but because we have caught the inner spirit or temper of His life. The spirit of His life has been handed down from generation to generation. It is a kind of contagion. One who has caught that spirit passes it on to another. To catch that spirit a man does not need to have any particular view about Jesus; indeed he does not even need to know that Jesus ever lived: all that he needs to do is to take into his life the peculiar spirit of Jesus' life no matter how it is mediated to him, no matter from what particular Christian he receives it, no matter whether he knows that it is the spirit of Jesus or has ever heard of Jesus at all. So, we are told in accordance with this view, that if a missionary is not permitted to proclaim Christ by his words he may at least proclaim Him by his life; he may be a true missionary merely by "living Christ" as distinguished from preaching Christ; those who come into contact with him can catch from him "the spirit of Jesus" or "the spirit of Christ" even if he is not allowed to tell them anything about the Cross of Christ or about the God in whom Jesus believed. And if people, through such missionaries, have caught the spirit of Jesus, what more could possibly be desired?

Such, carried to its logical conclusion, is the view which makes "the spirit of Jesus," in distinction from the Bible, the test of truth and of life.

What is wrong with it from the Christian point of

view? Many things, no doubt. But at the heart of what is wrong with it is this—that it ignores the fact of sin. All that we need, say the advocates of it, is to catch the spirit of Jesus. If we catch the spirit of Jesus, we can live the life that Jesus lived and then all will be well. Very different is what the real Christian says. The real Christian knows that unlike Jesus he is of himself under the guilt and power of sin, subject to the just wrath of God, unable to do any good, without hope save as Jesus has redeemed him by His precious blood. Can we catch the spirit of Jesus in the manner that is so glibly regarded as possible by those who have never been convicted of sin? Ah, no. We know only too well that we were dead in trespasses and sins, and that only as we have been made alive by the mysterious act of the Spirit of God can we even begin to be true followers of the holy Jesus.

These two things are poles apart. I do not think that there can be any clearness in our thinking so long as we confuse the one of them with the other. The man who thinks that all we need is to catch the spirit of Jesus and that we can catch that spirit without knowing what Jesus did for us on the cross and without the supernatural act of the Spirit of God in the new birth—that man takes Jesus as just a teacher and example. A Christian man, on the other hand, takes Jesus primarily as a Saviour. Where is He presented to us as our Saviour? The answer is, "In the whole Bible"; and that is the reason why the Bible is to us such a very precious book.

I have not time to speak at any length of other things which are being proposed as substitutes for the author-ity of the Bible. But before I leave you I do want to say just a word or two about one of these. It is the view that takes as the test of truth and of life the pronounce-ments and regulations of the Church.

Those who hold to this view as to the seat of author-ity do not usually deny the authority of the Bible in so many words. What they do is to say—by implication if not in words—that the Bible is interpreted authorita-tively by the "living Church." "When a man becomes a minister or a member of a Church," they say in effect, "it is his duty to support the program of that church. He may think that it is contrary to the Bible; but never mind, it is not his business in this particular matter to think; he must submit his judgment to the judgment of the councils of his church; he must let them interpret the Bible for him and must make the message that he supports conform to their shifting votes."

In sharp distinction from that view, we make the Bible, and the Bible only, the test of truth and of life. There is no living authority to interpret the Bible for us. We must read it every one for himself, and must ask God to help us as we read. A church that com-mands us to support any program on the authority of the decisions of the Church is usurping in the interests of fallible men an authority that belongs only to God.

But is it not a dangerous thing to reject other authorities in this fashion and submit ourselves unreservedly to the authority of this one Book? Yes, it is a very dangerous thing. It puts us sharply in conflict with the whole current of the age. But if it is a dangerous thing it is also a very blessed thing. It is a very blessed thing to hear the Word of the living God.

It is also a very blessed thing to proclaim that Word to others. Every Christian has the duty and the inestimable privilege of proclaiming it to others. But that duty and that privilege belong particularly to ministers.

What do you ministers do—if any of you are attending to me now—when you enter into your pulpits on Sunday mornings? Do you tell the people about your religious experiences; do you give them the benefit of your expert advice; do you express to them your views on the great questions of the day; do you make yourselves the promotion agents of some human organization? If these things are what you do, you may have very rich rewards, but there is one thing that you will miss. You may be great orators, but never will you be ministers of Jesus Christ. You may proclaim man's word with marvelous eloquence, but never can you proclaim the Word of God.

Oh, may God send us ministers of another kind! God grant that you, my brothers, may be ministers of another kind! May God send us ministers who come forth into their pulpits from a secret place of meditation and prayer, who are servants of Christ and not servants of men, who be they ever so humble are ambassadors of the King, who, as they stand behind the open Bible and expound its blessed words, can truly and honestly say, with Micaiah the son of Imlah: "As the Lord liveth, what the Lord saith unto me, that will I speak."

VIII

LIFE FOUNDED UPON TRUTH

HAVING considered with you the question what kind of book the Bible is, I think it is now high time that we should open up that book together and find out what is in it. We have shown that the Bible is worth reading, because it is the Word of God. Well, if it is worth reading, let us now begin to read it and see whether we can discover what it contains. What does the Bible teach?

I had in my mind a very good answer to that question when I was so very young as to have very little else in my mind. It is the answer to the third question in the Shorter Catechism, and it seems to me to be a very good thing. There are one hundred and six other good things in that Catechism. Those are the answers to the others of the one hundred and seven questions. I should certainly not go quite so far as to say what some Presbyterian is accused of having said—that the Shorter Catechism is more important than the Bible because the Shorter Catechism is "the Bible boiled down"—but all the same I am a convinced Presbyterian too, and I do maintain that the Shorter Catechism, with its marvelous comprehensiveness and its faithfulness to Scripture, with its solemnity and its tenderness, is the truest and noblest summary of what the Bible teaches that I have ever seen.

The third question in the Shorter Catechism is the question in which I am interested just now: "What do the Scriptures principally teach?" The answer is: "The Scriptures principally teach, what man is to believe concerning God, and what duty God requires of man."

The thing that I want you to notice about this answer is that it makes the Scriptures principally teach, first, what man is to believe and, second, what man is to do. It puts truth before conduct, doctrine before life. It makes truth the foundation of conduct and doctrine the foundation of life.

Today the order is commonly reversed. Life comes first, we are told, and doctrine comes afterwards. Religion is first an experience and only secondarily a doctrine. Doctrine is merely an expression of religious experience, and although the experience remains essentially the same its doctrinal expression must change as the generations pass. So, it is said, we value the great creeds of the Church not at all because we regard as true, in the plain man's sense of the word "true," the things that they contain, but because they expressed in the language of a by-gone day an experience which we can still share. So it is also, we are told, with the Bible. It is a great mistake, we are told, to take what the Bible says about Jesus as being true in the ordinary sense of the word "true"; but it is a still greater mistake to miss the experience which underlies what the Bible says. Thus when the Bible says that Jesus was born of a virgin, we do not, of course, it is said, believe that any physical miracle took place in connection with the birth of Jesus nineteen hundred years ago. But we do think that the men of that day were giving expression to something very precious when they said that, and we ought not to miss that very precious thing. Thus also, it is said, when people of long ago said that Jesus was God, they were of course meaning by that expression something that we do not at all accept. They meant that a heavenly person who had existed from all eternity came into this world by a voluntary act when Jesus of Nazareth was born. We do not at all believe that, say the persons whose views we are now summarizing; on the contrary, we believe that the person Jesus never existed before he was born in that Jewish family. Well, then, shall we just reject what those persons said when they declared Jesus to be God? Not at all, it is said. They were giving true expression, it is said, in the language of their day, to something that is just as precious to us as it was to them. They could not possibly give expression to it in any other language. If they had tried to give expression to it in our language, that would for them have been utterly false and futile. Do we then still believe in the deity of Christ? Oh, yes—

as the expression of a great experience. That experience is the really essential thing, but the intellectual expression of it must necessarily change from age to age.

Such is the attitude that is dominant in the religious world of our day—religion as an experience and doctrine as just the necessarily changing expression of the experience; life first and creed as just the changing expression of it. Those are the shibboleths that designate the prevailing attitude.

What shall we think of that attitude? Well, in the first place, I think we ought to face clearly the fact that it is an attitude of the most complete unbelief that could possibly be imagined. It denies not this truth or that but truth itself. It denies that there is any possibility of attaining to a truth which will always be true. There is truth, it holds, for this generation and truth for that generation, but no truth for all generations; there is truth for this race and truth for that race, but no truth for all races.

I remember some years ago that I read a paper at a conference of theological professors on the subject of "revelation." I read a paper and then another professor read a paper, and then still other professors made remarks about the papers. One of those latter professors said that although he disagreed with me completely, and agreed much more with my opponent, yet he was bound to say he thought that so far as the definition of terms was concerned I was a good deal nearer than my opponent to the historic meaning of the term "revelation." I thought that was very encouraging. But then he went on to say that even I did not mean the same thing by that term as people used to mean by it. Then he developed, with more or less clearness, the view that in general words are bound to change their meaning so that we never mean by the words that we use what past generations meant by them.

At any rate, whether that was what that particular professor said or not, I think it does represent what a good many people are saying. A good many people seem to think that every generation lives in a sort of intellectual water-tight compartment, without much chance of converse with other generations. Every generation has its own thought-forms and cannot by any chance use the thought-forms of any other generation. Do you know what I think of this notion? I think it comes very near being nonsense. If it were true, then books produced in past generations ought to be pure gibberish to us.

Take any book of Aristotle, for example. Aristotle lived some three and a half centuries before Christ. That book of Aristotle is composed of thousands of words. When Aristotle wrote the book it made sense, because the writer knew the meaning of every one of those thousands of words. Knowing the meaning of those words, he could fit them together so that the resulting book would make sense. But then, according to the theory with which we are now dealing, the meaning of every one of those words began to wobble, and has been wobbling for twenty-two centuries. Of course the words would not all wobble to just exactly the same extent and in exactly the same direction. That would be a chance too remote to be considered. The probabilities against it would be ten billion or more to one. Very well, then. What will inevitably be the result? The result, after twenty-two centuries of wobbling, will be that all those thousands of words will be completely out of alignment and the resulting book will be a meaningless jumble.

Yes, that will be the inevitable result if that professorial theory as to the inevitable shift in the meanings of words is correct. But the trouble is that that inevitable result is not the actual result. As a matter of fact, that book of Aristotle is just as limpidly clear and logical today as it ever was. What does that show? It shows that the theory that we have been dealing with is untrue. It shows that as a matter of fact words do not change their meaning in that kaleidoscopic way. It shows that there is an intellectual gold standard which enables us to carry on commerce perfectly well with the men of past generations.

What is true of different ages in the history of mankind is also true of different races co-existing today. People say that Western creeds ought not to be forced upon the Oriental mind. The Oriental mind, they say, ought to be allowed to go its own way and give its own expressions to the Christian faith. Well, I have examined one or two of those supposed expressions of the Oriental mind, and I am bound to say that they look to me uncommonly like the expressions of the mind of the South Side of Chicago. But how about it? Ought we to give our Western creeds to the Oriental mind? I shall just pass over the question whether those so-called Western creeds are really Western. Let us call them "Western creeds" in quotation marks and for the sake of the argument. Ought those Western creeds to be given to the Oriental mind? What is our answer?

The answer is: "Certainly." Of course those Western creeds ought to be given to the Oriental mind. But that ought to be done only on one condition—that those Western creeds are true. If they are not true, they ought not to be given to the Oriental mind or to any other kind of mind; but if they are true, they are just as true in China as they are in the United States.

The truth is that although I am thought by some of my friends to be very gullible, believing as I do that the Bible is true and that miracles really happened, there are some things about which I am a confirmed skeptic. Frankly, I do not believe in the separate existence of an Oriental mind or an Occidental mind or an ancient mind or a medieval mind or a modern mind. I do believe indeed that different races of mankind have different aptitudes or talents. It is perhaps true that French writers have the special gift of clearness, while Germans are characterized by a power of metaphysical speculation and by a certain solidity and thoroughness of learning. It must be admitted, indeed, that some German writers are admirably clear and some French writers, on the other hand, are awfully muddled. But still I suppose it is true to a very considerable extent that clearness is especially a French virtue of style. I have a great respect also for the intellectual gifts of Oriental peoples. I have no doubt but that those peoples are contributing something very valuable, and are going to contribute something still more valuable, to the intellectual life of the world.

But the really important thing is that under all fluctuations between this age and that age, between this nation and that nation, there is a gold standard of truth. We may misunderstand ancient writers, but our very recognition of the possibility of misunderstanding them shows that there is also a possibility of understanding them. I may have difficulty in understanding the mental processes of the Chinese and the Japanese, as they have difficulty in understanding mine; but the very fact that we can both detect that difficulty affords hope that the difficulty may be overcome, since the fact that we can detect that difficulty shows that there is a common intellectual ground upon which we can stand.

I think, therefore, that we can safely resist the bottomless skepticism which holds that all that remains constant from generation to generation is an experience that must clothe itself in ever-changing intellectual forms. I think that we may safely resist the skepticism which holds that the convictions of one generation can never by any chance be the convictions of another.

But are convictions important? Many people say that they are not. It does not make much difference, they say, what a man believes; life is the thing that counts. But merely saying a thing often does not make the thing true. As a matter of fact it does make a tremendous difference what a man believes.

A modern French novelist wrote in 1889 a very interesting book to show that that is the case. I have just been re-reading it, and I find it almost as impressive as I found it when I read it the first time. The novelist who wrote it is hardly to be put in the first rank of French writers. But this one book of his is certainly worth reading. Some years ago I was talking about it to a French lecturer and critic who was inclined to be very severe upon this writer. But then I said that I had read one book of this writer and that it seemed to my poor judgment to be a masterpiece. "Yes," said the critic with whom I was talking; "that particular book of this writer is indeed a masterpiece." The book that I am referring to is the novel by Paul Bourget entitled *Le Disciple*, "The Disciple." It describes, with a delicacy of touch in which French writers excel, the simple and austere life of a noted philosopher and psychologist.

He was engrossed altogether in the things of the mind. His lodging was up four flights of stairs. His daily existence was an invariable routine. Coffee at six o'clock, lunch or breakfast at ten, walk until noon, work again until four, visits of scholars and students three times a week from four to six, dinner at six, short walk, work, bed promptly at ten. An inoffensive, scholarly man if there ever was one, a man who, in the words of his caretaker, "wouldn't hurt a fly."

But one day this peaceful routine was strangely broken into. The philosopher was summoned to a criminal inquest. A former pupil of his was accused of murder. He had been a brilliant young man, who had climbed those four flights of stairs full of enthusiasm for what he regarded as liberating doctrines. He had drunk in those doctrines only too well. In the prison he wrote an account of his life for the eye of his revered master. In it the abstract becomes concrete. The terrible story is told of the way in which those supposedly liberating doctrines work out in actual practice.

It is rather a tremendous little book—that study of "The Disciple" by Paul Bourget.

But the same tragedy as that which is so powerfully depicted in that little book is appearing on a gigantic scale in the whole history of our times. Fifty or even twenty-five years ago, certain views about God and about the Bible might have seemed to a superficial observer to be perfectly respectable and perfectly innocent—as harmless and as remote from anything like tragedy as Bourget's philosopher up his four flights of stairs. It was such a sweet, pleasant thing—that older Modernism, or "Liberalism," as it was euphemistically called. But today it is having its perfect work. It is destroying civil and religious liberty; it is defiling the sweetness and gentleness of the Christian home; it is causing contracts public and private to be explained away, until the man or the nation that sweareth to his own hurt and changeth not is regarded as a curious relic of the past. Do you look with complacency upon this world where purity and honesty and liberty are regarded as out of date? Do you think it is going to be a pleasant world to live in? If you do, you are blind. You have to be pretty blind not to see that mankind is today standing over an abyss.

Do not be deceived, my friends. This notion that it does not make much difference what a man believes, this notion that doctrine is unimportant and that life comes first, is one of the most devilish errors that are to be found in the whole of Satan's arsenal. How many human lives it has wrecked, how many mothers' hearts it has broken! That French novelist is entirely right. Out of the Pandora box of highly respectable philosophy come murders, adulteries, lies and every evil thing.

Well, I have been talking about various things. It might look as though I had forgotten all about the thing I started out to talk about. It might look as though I had forgotten all about the Bible. But indeed that is not the case. I have been talking about these other things, I have been talking about the snarl into which men have come, only in order that at the last I may lead you to the place where that snarl may be straightened out. What does the Bible say about the question that we have been discussing this afternoon? What does the Bible say about the question whether doctrine is merely the changing expression of life or whether—the other way around—life is founded upon doctrine?

You do not have to read very far in the Bible in order to get the answer. The answer is given to you in the first verse. Does the Bible begin with exhortation; does it begin with a program of life? No, it begins with a doctrine. "In the beginning God created the heaven and the earth." That is the foundation doctrine upon which everything else that the Bible says is based.

The Bible does present a way of life; it tells men the way in which they ought to live. But always when it does so it grounds that way of life in truth.

Run through the Bible in your minds, my friends, and see whether I am not right.

In the Old Testament a wonderful program of life is presented. It is called the Ten Commandments. But do the Ten Commandments begin with commandments? Not at all. They begin with doctrine. "I am the

Lord thy God, which have brought thee out of the land of Egypt, out of the house of bondage." That is the preface to the Ten Commandments. It is not a commandment. It is not a program. It is a doctrine. Only because that doctrine is true—only because the one speaking in the commandments is the Lord God—have the commandments any authority.

The Old Testament contains another wonderful presentation of the way in which men should live. Like the Ten Commandments it was quoted by Jesus. It reads: "Thou shalt love the Lord thy God with all thine heart, and with all thy soul, and with all thy might." That is a wonderful commandment indeed—that commandment of love. But does it begin with a commandment? Not at all. It begins with a doctrine. It is grounded upon a doctrine. "Hear, O Israel," says the passage in Deuteronomy: "The Lord our God is one Lord, And thou shalt love the Lord thy God with all thine heart, and with all thy soul, and with all thy might." Only because that doctrine is true has the commandment any meaning. Only because there is one God only and only because that one God is Jehovah are God's people commanded to love that one God with all their heart and soul and might.

Turn then to the New Testament. The New Testament tells us how Jesus came. Did He come in the modern fashion telling people that it made no difference what they believed and that the thing for them to do was just to live the life first and then afterwards give doctrinal expression to the life?

Well, He did come presenting to them a life that they should live. "Repent," He said, when He came forward in His public ministry in Galilee. But is that all that He said? Did He just say: "Repent, repent, repent, repent, repent"? Not at all. He said: "Repent: for the kingdom of heaven is at hand." "The kingdom of heaven is at hand" is not a command or a program. It is a doctrine; and upon that doctrine the command of Jesus to repent is based.

Jesus sat one day by the well, and talked to a sinful woman. In the course of the conversation He laid His finger upon the sore spot in that woman's life. "Thou hast had five husbands," He said; "and he whom thou now hast is not thy husband." Then, apparently to evade the disconcerting question of the sin in her own life, the woman asked Jesus a theological question about the right place in which to worship God—whether on Mount Gerizim or in Jerusalem. What did Jesus do with that woman's theological question? Did He brush it aside after the manner of certain modern religious workers? Did He say: "You are evading the real question; we will take up your theological question afterwards, but now let us come back to the question of the sin in your own life." No, He did nothing of the kind. He answered that woman's theological question with the utmost fulness as though the woman's soul· depended on her getting the right answer. Not Gerizim, He said, but Jerusalem is the place in which to worship God, but the time is coming when the worship of God will be bound to no set places. And then, in response to that sinful, unconverted woman's question Jesus engaged in some of the profoundest theological teaching in the whole of the Bible. Apparently Jesus regarded a right doctrine of God not as something that comes along after salvation but as something necessary to salvation.

At the beginning of the Book of Acts Jesus is said to have told His disciples to be witnesses unto Him. On the day of Pentecost, a few days later, Peter arose to obey that command. He preached that great sermon which is found in the second chapter of Acts. What did he say in that sermon? He had not had some advantages which men have today. He had not had the inestimable advantage of modern "religious education." If he had had, no doubt he would have told the people that it did not make any difference what doctrine they held about Jesus or about anything else, and that life was the only thing that mattered. But poor Peter! He had not had the advantage of modern religious education. He had to content himself with another advantage—he had just been filled with the Holy Ghost. The result is that his sermon is doctrinal through and through. He just gave them the facts about Jesus. Not a bit of exhortation, nothing about a program. Just facts, facts, facts, doctrine, doctrine, doctrine. What was the result? They were "pricked in their hearts." Then Peter told them what to do. Three thousand were saved.

So it is everywhere in the Bible, my friends. First doctrine, then life. The Bible from Genesis to Revelation gives not a bit of comfort to the skeptical notion that doctrine is the mere changing and symbolic expression of Christian experience. The Bible founds living everywhere squarely upon truth. God grant that you may all receive that truth for the saving of your souls, and that having been saved you may live true Christian lives upon this earth and then live in God's presence for evermore!

IX

GOD, THE CREATOR

WE have seen that the Bible is doctrinal through and
through. It gives not the slightest bit of comfort to the
skeptical notion, so much in vogue today, that doctrine
is merely the necessarily changing form in which Christian experience expresses itself. The Bible, unlike this
skepticism, grounds life squarely in truth. Christianity,
according to the Bible, is not a life as distinguished
from a doctrine and it is not a life that has doctrine as
its changing expression, but—just the other way around
—it is a life founded upon a doctrine.

That doctrine upon which the Bible grounds life is
not one isolated doctrine, and it is not a mere series of
doctrines, but it is a system of doctrine. If the Bible
contained a number of divergent systems, it could not
possibly be the Word of God, because it could not possibly be true throughout. The ordination pledge to
which all ministers and elders in the Presbyterian
Church in the U. S. A. have subscribed is quite right in
speaking of *the* system of doctrine taught in the Holy
Scriptures.

I think great stress ought to be laid upon that fact.

A great deal of harm is done when people take one part of the teaching of the Bible out of its connection with the rest, or when they leave gaps in their presentation of what the Bible teaches. It is very important to see that the Bible does far more than present isolated truths. It is very important to see that it presents a system of truth, and it is very important to view that system not in part but as a whole.

As we study that system here together, let us remember above all things that it is not a system which man has devised, but a system which God has revealed—revealed graciously in His holy Word.

Where shall we begin in our study of that great system of revealed truth that the Bible contains? I think we ought to begin where the Bible begins. I think we ought to begin with a consideration of what the Bible teaches about God as the Creator and Ruler of the world.

There are many today who insist that we ought to begin at another place. There are many who tell us that we ought to begin with a consideration of the human life of Jesus. In fact these people often tell us that that is where we ought not only to begin but also to end. They are telling us that that is all we really need to know.

All that we need to know about God, they tell us, is that God is like Jesus. We do not need to know how the universe came into being, they tell us, or whether there is a God who governs it in its course. These things belong to metaphysics, they say, not to religion. We are not interested, they say, in the question whether God is powerful, but are only interested in conceiving of Him as good.

Such is the view of those who use the phrase "the Christlike God." That phrase, as it is commonly used, grates upon Christian ears. It grates upon the ears of those who believe not that God is *like* Jesus, but that Jesus Himself *is* God.

But what is wrong with that view? Aside from the terminology that is used to set it forth, what is wrong with the view itself? What is wrong with this notion that all that we know about God is that He possesses the moral excellencies that are found in the man Jesus?

Two things at least are wrong with it. In the first place, it is terribly degrading to Jesus. That may seem strange at first sight. It may seem strange that a view which holds that all we need to know about God is that God is like Jesus should be derogatory to Jesus, but a little reflection will show that it *is* derogatory to Jesus in the extreme.

It is derogatory to Jesus because it does despite to the deepest things in Jesus' teaching and example. At the very heart of the life of Jesus was just that view of God which is being so contemptuously rejected by those who say that the moral life of the man Jesus tells us all that we need to know about God.

Jesus certainly believed that God is the Creator and Ruler of the universe, and that belief belonged to the foundation of everything that He believed. Not a sparrow, He said to His disciples, shall "fall on the ground without your Father." It is God, according to Jesus, who clothes the lilies of the field, and it is God who makes the sun to rise on just and unjust. There can be no doubt whatever but that Jesus held just that view of God which the persons of whom we have been speaking reject as being mere metaphysics. He put at the very foundation of His teaching and His life that divinely revealed metaphysic which is found in the first verse of Genesis. Everything that He did, with everything that He said, was based upon the great truth: "In the beginning God created the heaven and the earth." God, according to Jesus, is the Creator and the absolute Ruler of the universe, bringing all things to pass in accordance with the counsel of His will. You may not like that view of God, but if you are a historian who sees things as they are you will be obliged to recognize the fact that it was certainly the view held by Jesus of Nazareth.

Moreover, Jesus certainly held that men had a true knowledge of God before He appeared upon the earth. He held that they had that true knowledge of God from the Old Testament. We have already observed in previous talks in this little series that Jesus regarded the Old Testament as the very Word of God and that He put that conviction about the Old Testament at the very heart both of His teaching and of His life. How, then, if you reject that conviction, can you possibly think that you are doing honor to Jesus? If you hold that the revelation of God contained in the Old Testament is valueless and that all that we need to know about God is found in the moral character of the man Jesus of Nazareth, what will you do with the fact that the Jesus to whom you appeal put at the very basis of that moral character which you so much admire a view of the Old Testament and a view of God which you contemptuously reject?

Jesus did, indeed, present Himself as revealing God and as being in His very person the revelation of God. "He that hath seen me," He said, "hath seen the Father; and how sayest thou then, Shew us the Father?" But that certainly does not mean that the disciples who were with our Lord on earth were told by our Lord suddenly to regard as of no value the knowledge of God which they already had. The key to what our Lord meant when He said, "He that hath seen me hath seen the Father" is to be found, I am inclined to think, in the words in John 1:18: "No man hath seen God at any time; God only begotten, which is in the bosom of the Father, he hath declared Him." Devout readers of the Old Testament had *known* God, but they had not seen Him, since God is invisible. But now the one who is both God and only-begotten, the eternal Son, has become flesh, and because He has become flesh can actually be seen with men's eyes. A man who sees Him sees the Father, since He is Himself one in substance with the Father. Thus, in Christ, the longing of men actually to *see* God is satisfied.

At any rate, what is perfectly clear is that everywhere Jesus presupposed the knowledge of God which His disciples had from the Old Testament. He just assumes that His disciples have that knowledge, and then, building upon that knowledge He leads them on into a fuller and more glorious knowledge through His intercourse with them upon earth.

To hold, then, that all that we need to know about God is found in the moral character of the man Jesus of Nazareth, and that we can be indifferent to the question whether God is the Maker and Ruler of the world, is to treat Jesus Himself with contempt, since it means that we reject what He himself put at the very foundation of His life and of His teaching.

But that view is not only derogatory to Jesus. It is also derogatory to God. What a low view of God it is to be sure when men say that they are not interested in the question whether He is powerful, whether He is the Creator or Ruler of the world, but are only interested in the question whether He is good!

Is that view of God really right? [1] Has all our trust

[1] The treatment of this question in the following paragraphs is similar to that in the book by the same writer, *What Is Faith?"* 1925, pp. 60 f.

in the infinite power of our God been wrong when in the midst of storms and trials and a host of enemies we have quoted the words of Scripture: "If God be for us, who can be against us?" Was Isaiah wrong when he turned his eyes to the starry heavens and said: "Lift up your eyes on high, and behold who hath created these things, that bringeth out their host by number: he calleth them all by names by the greatness of his might, for that he is strong in power; not one faileth"? Was Jesus wrong when He bade His disciples trust in Him who clothes the lilies of the field and when He said: "Fear not, little flock; for it is your Father's good pleasure to give you the kingdom"?

To these questions philosophers may return this answer or that, but the answer of the Christian heart is plain. Away with all these pale abstractions, it cries; away with this strange theory that speaks of the goodness of God but deprives Him of His power! If God is good only and not powerful, we are of all men most miserable. We had trusted Him so implicitly; we had felt so safe in His everlasting arms. But now you tell us that our confidence was misplaced and that God really had no power to save His children when they call! Shall we believe you? Ah, no, my friends. Not if we are Christians. Others may heed these voices that bid us lose confidence in the power of our God, but as for us Christians, we will say still, though ten million times ten million universes unloose against us all their

mighty power, though we stand amid the clash of fall-
ing systems and contemplate a universal ruin—we will
say still that it is God's world which He can create and
He destroy, and that through Christ's grace we are
safe forever in the arms of our heavenly Father.

But, people say, even if God is not thus all-powerful,
even if we can no longer think of Him as the sovereign
Creator and Ruler of the world, even if we relegate
these things to the realm of mere metaphysics, have we
not at least something left? Have we not goodness left?
We do not know how the world came into being; we
do not know what will be our fate when we pass
through the dark portals of death. But can we not find
a higher and more disinterested worship—far higher,
it would seem than that which Jesus practised—in the
reverence for goodness stripped of the old vulgar trappings of power?

It sounds noble at first. But consider it for a moment
and its glory turns to ashes and leaves us in despair.
What is meant by a goodness that has no power? Is not
goodness a mere abstraction except as it belongs to persons? As does not the very notion of a person involve
the power to act? Goodness altogether divorced from
power is therefore no goodness at all. The truth is that
if you try to make God good only and not powerful,
both God and goodness have been destroyed.

We insist then that in order to know God it is not
sufficient to examine the moral life of the man Jesus of

Nazareth. To regard that as sufficient is to do despite to Jesus Himself, and it leaves us with a God who is no God at all.

What then is the view of God which the Bible presents to us, when we take the Bible—as we ought to take it—as a whole?

If you will let me answer that question in one word, and if you will not forbid me to make that one word a convenient word which philosophers use, I will just say that the view of God which the Bible presents is the view which philosophers call "theism"—that is, it is the view which holds that there is a personal God who is Creator and Ruler of the world. That is the view which Jesus presents with particular clearness, and that is the view which the Bible presents as a whole.

To understand just what that view of God is, we cannot do better than contrast it with two other views which men have often held.

In the first place, there is the view called deism. According to that view, God created the universe, but then left it alone to run by itself like a machine. That view, affirming the existence of a personal God but denying His presence in the world and His active governance of it, used to be held widely by unbelievers of past generations; but today it is dead. I do not know whether there are any real deists at the present time.

A second error is, however, very much alive; in fact, in different forms, and with greater or less modification, it is the view underlying the Modernism that is stifling the life of such large portions of the Church today. That is the ancient error called "pantheism." It is held in very many different forms, and with many degrees of consistency. According to the strict meaning of the term, it is the view that "all is God," the view that simply identifies God with the totality of existing things.

I suppose the first impulse of the ordinary man, untrained in philosophy, is to regard that view as absurd. It was in that way that I regarded it when I first heard of it when I was at school or college. It seemed to me almost more preposterous than the idolatry of the heathen who bows down to idols of wood and stone.

But here is the strange thing, my friends—a great many people who regard pantheism as wrong if the meaning of the term is explained to them are practically pantheists themselves. They are not aware of the fact, but they are pantheists all the same.[2]

We find ourselves in the midst of the mighty process of nature. It manifests itself in the wonders of the starry heavens and the equal wonders that the interior of the atom now reveals. It is seen in the revolving seasons and also in the achievements of the human mind. In the presence of that mighty process of nature, we stand in awe; we are impressed with our own little-

[2] The treatment of this subject in the following three paragraphs is similar to that in *What Is Faith?* pp. 70 f.

ness; we understand that we are but infinitesimal parts of a mighty whole. And to that mighty whole, to that stupendous world-process, whose vastness we moderns have come to understand as never before, the pantheist applies the dread name of God. God is thus no longer thought of as an artificer apart from his machine; He is thought of rather as the universe itself, conceived of not in its individual manifestations but as a mighty whole.

Such is pantheism in the strict sense of the word. We can well understand the appeal which such a view has for many minds. It has stimulated some of the most brilliant thinking and inspired some of the grandest poetry of the race.

But it contains no comfort whatever for oppressed and burdened souls. If God be merely another name for the totality of things, then if we possess Him we have nothing that we did not have before. There is for us now no more appeal from nature to nature's God. We are now nothing but the playthings of blind force.

Feeling, perhaps, the defects of the stark pantheism which identifies God with all that exists, some men have sought for a "higher pantheism" of various kinds. No, they say to themselves, God is not simply another name for the universe as a whole, but is to be identified rather with the spiritual purpose that runs through the universe. Some of them have said that God is the soul of the universe. As the human body has a human soul, so the universe has a soul, they say, and that soul is to be called "God."

Two profound defects are found in all these forms of pantheism, high and middling and low. In the first place, they give us a God who is in some kind of necessary connection with the world. Not only does the world not exist apart from God, they tell us, but God does not exist apart from the world. What becomes, then, of the holiness or separateness of God? Clothe such a view with all the beauty of language with which it has been celebrated by poets and philosophers, and still it gives us a God who is merely a function or an aspect of the world. Such a God can never bring us into contact with that dread and mysterious realm of the beyond into which our souls long to enter.

In the second place, pantheism high or low can never really give us a personal God. A God of which we are parts can never be a God with whom we can have communion. We can never stand in the presence of such a God as one person stands in the presence of another. We can never say "Thou" to such a God, and such a God can never say "Thou" to us. We can never love such a God, and such a God can never love us. An abstraction can neither love nor be loved. Never could we say to a "world process" or to a "spiritual meaning" or to a principle of goodness: "Our Father which art in heaven."

How gloriously are those two defects of pantheism avoided in the teaching of Holy Scripture!

The former of the two defects is certainly avoided. What is it that stands out sharply in the Bible from beginning to end? Is it not the awful holiness or separateness of God, the awful distinction between the finite and the infinite, between the creature and the Creator?

The Bible does indeed teach us that God is immanent in the world. He is not a God afar off. He is not a God who stands aloof from the universe as an artificer stands aloof from his machine. The devout reader of the Bible can say with Tennyson: "Closer is He than breathing, and nearer than hands and feet."

But if God is thus immanent in the world, He is also transcendent. The world is dependent upon Him, but He is not dependent upon the world. He has set bounds to the world, but the world has set no bounds to Him. It is the work of His hands, but He is from eternity. "Before the mountains were brought forth, or ever thou hadst formed the earth and the world, even from everlasting to everlasting, thou art God." Running all through the Bible is the awful separateness of God from the world. That is what the Bible calls the holiness of God. The Bible, unlike the pantheists, presents to us a holy God.

But the Bible also—and again unlike the pantheists—presents to us a personal God. The God of the Bible is not just another name for the universe itself, nor is He a name for a spiritual purpose supposed to run through the universe, or for any impersonal principle of goodness. No, He is a person. That much is clear at the start. We shall speak in a subsequent talk of the deeper mystery of the three persons in one God. But at least it is clear that God is personal. He is not a force or a principle or a collective somewhat of which we are parts. He is a person, to whom we can say "Thou," a person who can, if He will, speak to us as a man speaketh to His friend, and who can, if He will, become to us a heavenly Father.

But what is needed first of all is that we shall stand in awe before His throne. We are living in an age when men have forgotten God. They have become engrossed in their own affairs. They have been puffed up in their pride. They have put God out of their thoughts. The result is that our boasted civilization is rushing rapidly to its fall. Oh, that men would turn to God while yet there is time!

How is it with you, my friends? Have you been walking in your own paths? Have you forgotten God? If so, I bid you read the blessed book that will tell you how He may be found. If you heed His Word you may first stand in awe before His throne, and then, by the way that He has provided, you may come to be at peace with Him and be His child for evermore.

X

THE TRIUNE GOD

IN this little series of talks we spent some time discussing the question what kind of book the Bible is; but at last we plunged fairly into the question what that book teaches. We were talking about what the Bible teaches regarding God.

In dealing with that subject, we had not time to do any more than make a beginning. All that we had time to do was to observe that the Bible tells us there is a personal God, Creator and Ruler of the World. God, according to the Bible, is not another name for the mighty process of nature, and He is not some one part or aspect of that process, but He is a free and holy person, who created the process of nature by the fiat of His will and who is eternally independent of the universe that He has made.

Now we ask more in detail what the Bible tells us about God. When we ask that, I know we shall be met with an objection. We are seeking to know God. Well, there are many people who tell us that we ought not to seek to know God. The knowledge of God, they say, is the death of religion. Instead of seeking to know

God, they tell us, we ought simply to feel Him; putting all theology aside, they say, we ought just to sink ourselves in the boundless ocean of God's being.[1]

Such is the attitude of the mystics ancient and modern. But it is not the attitude of the Christian. The Christian, unlike the mystic, knows Him whom He has believed.

What shall be said of a religion that depreciates theology, that depreciates the knowledge of God?

One thing that can be said of it is that it hardly possesses any moral quality at all. Pure feeling, if such a thing exists, is non-moral. That can be observed in the sphere of human relationships. What makes my affection for a human friend such an ennobling thing is the knowledge that I have of the character and the needs of my friend. Am I indifferent to such knowledge? Am I indifferent to an error that seeks to contravene it? Am I indifferent to base slanders which are directed against my friend's reputation? Not if I am a friend worthy of the name. Human affection, apparently so simple, is in reality just bristling with doctrine; it depends upon a host of observations, stored up in the mind, regarding the object of the affection.

That is true, I think, even with regard to those human affections that are often thought of as instinctive. Take, for example, the love of a mother for a child.

---

[1] The following treatment of this objection is similar to the treatment by the same writer in *Christianity and Liberalism*, 1923, pp. 54 f.

That love is no doubt independent of excellence in the child; it is impossible to kill a mother's love, no matter what one may do. But is a mother's love independent of some knowledge of the child, independent of some knowledge of the child's sufferings and needs, independent of some ability to enter into the soul of the child in order to sympathize and understand? If it is thus independent of all knowledge, I am inclined to think that it is hardly human affection at all; it has descended to an almost sub-human level.

It is to that sub-human, non-personal level that the mystic seeks to degrade our communion with God. Very different is the love of God as the Bible sets it forth. According to the Bible, we love God because He first loved us; and He has told us of His love in His holy Word. We love God, if we obey what the Bible tells us, because God has made Himself known to us and has thus shown Himself to be worthy of our love.

I do not mean to say that the Christian in his communion with God is always rehearsing consciously the things that God has told us about Himself. There are times, as someone has observed, when a child of God, weary with the battle of life, can say only, as he lies down to rest: "Lord, Thou knowest, we are on the same old terms." There are times when the Christian can be strangely conscious of the presence of God, even though he is not for the moment thinking in detail about the things that he knows regarding God. Certainly the

Bible does offer to us an immediate communion with God, which is like no other experience which a man can possibly have; and certainly the Bible does make a distinction between knowing God and merely knowing about God. But underlying that sweet and blessed communion of the Christian with his God there is a true knowledge of God. A communion with God which is independent of that knowledge of God is communion with some other god and not with the living and true God whom the Bible reveals.

Every true man is resentful of slanders against a human friend. Should we not be grieved ten times more by slanders against our God? How can we possibly listen with polite complacency, then, when men break down the distinction between God and man, and drag God down to man's level? How can we possibly say, as in one way or another is so often said, that orthodoxy makes little difference. We should never talk in any such way about a human friend. We should never say with regard to a human friend that it makes no difference whether our view of him is right or wrong. How, then, can we say that absurd thing with regard to God?

The really consistent Christian can have nothing whatever to do with such doctrinal indifferentism. There is nothing so dishonoring to God, he will say, as to be indifferent to the things that God has told us about Himself in His holy Word.

What, then, has God told us about Himself in His

Word? I certainly cannot now answer that question with any fulness. But there are a few things that I do want to say, and if by saying them I can be helpful to you in your own reading of the Bible, the purpose of this little series of talks will have been attained.

In the Shorter Catechism of the Presbyterian churches, there is the following answer to the question, "What is God?":

"God is a Spirit, infinite, eternal, and unchangeable, in His being, wisdom, power, holiness, justice, goodness, and truth."

That answer is certainly in accordance with the Bible. I think it will help us a little bit to get straight in our minds what the Bible says about God.

Notice that God is here said to be infinite, eternal and unchangeable. What is meant by saying that He is infinite? Well, the word "infinite" means without an end or a limit. Other beings are limited: God is unlimited. I suppose it is easy for us to fall into our ordinary spatial conceptions in trying to think of God. We may imagine ourselves passing from the earth to the remotest star known to modern astronomy—many, many light-years away. Well, when we have got there, we are not one slightest fraction of an inch nearer to fathoming infinity than we were when we started. We might imagine ourselves traveling ten million times ten million times farther still, and still we should not be any nearer to infinity than when we started. We cannot conceive a limit to space, but neither can we conceive of infinite space. Our mind faints in the presence of infinity.

But we were really wrong in using those spatial conceptions in thinking of infinity, and particularly wrong were we in using spatial conceptions in thinking of the infinite God. It may help us to the threshold of the truth to say that God pervades the whole vast area of the universe known to science, and then infinitely more; it may help us to the threshold of the truth to say that God inhabits infinite space: but when we look a little deeper we see that space itself belongs to finite things and that the notion of infinite space is without meaning. God created space when He created finite things. He Himself is beyond space. There is no near and no far to Him. Everything to Him is equally near.

So it is when we try to think of God as eternal. If the word "infinity" is related, by way of contrast, to the notion of space, so the word "eternity" is related, by way of contrast, to the notion of time. When we say that God is eternal, we mean that He had no beginning and that He will have no end. But we really mean more than that. We mean that time has no meaning for Him, save as it has meaning to the creatures whom He has made. He created time, when He created finite creatures. He himself is beyond time. There is no past and no future to Him. The Bible puts that in poetical language when it says: "For a thousand years in thy sight are as yesterday when it is past, and as a watch in the night." We of course are obliged to think of the actions of God as taking place in time. We are obliged to think of Him as doing one thing after another thing; we are obliged to think of Him as doing this today and that tomorrow. We have a perfect right so to think, and the Bible amply confirms us in that right. To us there is indeed such a thing as past and present and future, and when God deals with us He acts in a truly temporal series. But to God Himself all things are equally present. There is no such thing as "before" or "after" to Him.

It is very important to see clearly that God is thus infinite, eternal and unchangeable. These attributes of God are often denied. Those who have denied them have told us that God is a finite God. We must not blame Him, they tell us, if things are not just right in the world. He is doing the best He can, they say; He is trying to bring order out of chaos, but He is faced by a recalcitrant material which He did not create and which He can mould only gradually and imperfectly to His will. It is our business to help Him, and while we may at first sight regret that we have not the all-powerful God that we used to think we had, yet we can comfort ourselves with the inspiring thought that the God that we do have needs our help and indeed cannot do without it.

What shall we say of such a finite God? I will tell

you plainly what I think we ought to say about Him. He is not God but *a* god. He is a product of men's thoughts. Men have made many such little gods. Of the making of gods, as of the making of books, there is no end. But, as for us Christians, with our Bibles before us, we turn from all such little gods of man's making, out toward the dread mystery of the infinite and eternal, and say, as Augustine said, with a holy fear: "Thou hast made us for thyself, and our heart is restless until it finds its rest in thee."

The definition in the Shorter Catechism, which we are taking to give us our outline of what the Bible tells us about God, says not only that God is infinite, eternal and unchangeable in His being and in His power and in His holiness, but also that He is infinite, eternal and unchangeable in His wisdom and in His justice, goodness and truth.

Does that seem surprising to you in the light of what we have just been saying? Well, perhaps it might seem to be surprising. These qualities—wisdom, justice, goodness and truth—are such startlingly human qualities. Can we ascribe them to that infinite, eternal and unchangeable God of whom we have just been speaking? If we do try to ascribe them to that God, are we not guilty of a naïve anthropomorphism? Are we not guilty of the childish error of thinking of God as though He were just a big man up in the sky? Are we not guilty of making a god in our own image?

The answer is: No, we are not guilty of that. If we think of God as having some attributes which we also possess, we may conceivably be doing it for one or the other of two reasons. In the first place, we may be doing it because we are making God in our own image. But, in the second place, we may be doing it because God has made us in His image.

The Bible tells us that this second alternative is correct. God made man in the image of God, and that is the reason why God possesses some attributes which man also possesses, though God possesses them to an infinitely higher degree.

The Bible is not afraid of speaking of God in a startlingly tender and human sort of way. It does so just in passages where the majesty of God is set forth. "It is he that sitteth upon the circle of the earth," says the fortieth chapter of Isaiah, "and the inhabitants thereof are as grasshoppers." "All nations before him are as nothing; and they are counted to him less than nothing, and vanity." But what says that same fortieth chapter of Isaiah about this same terrible God? Here is what it says: "He shall feed his flock like a shepherd: he shall gather the lambs with his arm, and carry them in his bosom, and shall gently lead those that are with young."

How wonderfully the Bible sets forth the tenderness of God! Is that merely figurative? Are we wrong in thinking of God in such childlike fashion? Many philosophers say so. They will not think of God as a person. Oh, no. That would be dragging Him down too much to our level! So they make of Him a pale abstraction. The Bible seems childish to them in the warm, personal way in which it speaks of God.

Are those philosophers right or is the Bible right? Thank God, the Bible is right, my friends. The philosophers despise children who think of God as their heavenly Father. But the philosophers are wrong and the children are right. Did not our Lord Jesus say: "I thank thee, O Father, Lord of heaven and earth, because thou hast hid these things from the wise and prudent, and hast revealed them unto babes."

No, God is no pale abstraction. He is a person. That simple truth—precious possession of simple souls—is more profound than all the philosophies of all the ages.

But now we come to a great mystery. God, according to the Bible, is not just one person, but He is three persons in one God. That is the great mystery of the Trinity.

The Trinity is revealed to us only in the Bible. We said at the beginning of this little series of talks that God has revealed some things to us through nature and through conscience. But the Trinity is not among them. This He has revealed to us by supernatural revelation and by supernatural revelation alone.

We can, it is true, detect something in the doctrine of the Trinity that serves to render clearer and richer even what nature and conscience reveal. Nature and conscience reveal, in a revelation which, it is true, sinful man seldom receives, a personal and holy God, Creator of the world. But how can a personal and holy being exist entirely alone? The thing is difficult for us to understand. That difficulty is wonderfully overcome by the doctrine of the Trinity, which tells us that even before God had created the world there was a personal inter-relation within the Godhead.

But we ought to be exceedingly cautious about such considerations. Though God is a person, He is a person very different from us finite persons, and I am not sure that we could ever have said, on the basis of any general revelation in nature and conscience, that an infinite person could not have existed entirely alone. Let us put such considerations, then, aside. When we are engaging in them we are venturing upon holy ground, where we can walk at best with but trembling and halting footsteps. The thing that is perfectly clear is that we should not have had any real knowledge of the holy mystery of the Trinity had not that mystery been revealed to us in the written Word of God.

Within the Word of God, it is in the New Testament that the doctrine of the Trinity is taught. There are hints of it in the Old Testament, but they are only hints, and it was left to the New Testament for this precious doctrine to be clearly revealed.

In the New Testament, the doctrine is taught with

the utmost clearness; and, as has well been pointed out by Dr. B. B. Warfield, in a splendid article on the Trinity,[2] the doctrine is presupposed even more than it is expressly taught. That is, the New Testament is founded throughout on the doctrine of the Trinity, and the doctrine was really established by the great facts of the incarnation of the Son of God and the work of the Holy Spirit even before it was enunciated in words.

Only the smallest part of the teaching of the New Testament about the Trinity is found in passages where the doctrine is stated as a whole. What the New Testament ordinarily does is to state parts of the doctrine, so that when we put those parts together, and when we summarize them, we have the great doctrine of the three persons and one God.

For example, all passages in the New Testament where the deity of Jesus Christ is set forth are, when taken in connection with passages setting forth the deity and personality of the Holy Spirit, passages supporting the doctrine of the Trinity. In the next talk, I hope to deal with some of those passages.

But what needs to be observed now is that although by far the larger part of the Biblical teaching about the Trinity is given in that incidental and partial way—presupposing the doctrine rather than formally enunciating

---

[2] B. B. Warfield, Article, "Trinity," in *International Standard Bible Encyclopedia*, now reprinted in his collected works, in the volume *Biblical Doctrines*, 1929, pp. 143-147. The present writer is much indebted to that article for the treatment of this whole subject.

it as a whole—yet there are some passages where the doctrine is definitely presented by the mention, together, of Father, Son and Holy Ghost.

The most famous of such passages, I suppose, is found in the Great Commission, given by the risen Lord to His disciples according to the twenty-eighth chapter of Matthew. "Go ye therefore, and teach all nations, baptizing them in the name of the Father, and of the Son, and of the Holy Ghost." There we have a mention of all three persons of the Trinity in the most complete coördination and equality—yet all three persons are plainly not three Gods but one. Here, in this solemn Commission by our Lord, the God of all true Christians is forever designated as a triune God.

We think also, for example, of the apostolic benediction at the end of the Second Epistle to the Corinthians: "The grace of the Lord Jesus Christ, and the love of God, and the communion of the Holy Ghost, be with you all." Here the terminology is a little different from that in the Great Commission. Paul speaks of the Son as "the Lord." But the word "Lord" in the Pauline Epistles is plainly a designation of deity, like the other Greek word which is translated into English by the word "God." It is the Greek word used to translate the holy name of God, "Jehovah," in the Greek translation of the Old Testament which Paul used, and Paul does not hesitate to apply to Christ Old Testament passages which speak of Jehovah.

That brings us to something supremely important in the teaching of the whole New Testament about the Trinity. It is this—that the New Testament writers, in presenting God as triune, are never for one moment conscious of saying anything that could by any possibility be regarded as contradicting the Old Testament teaching that there is but one God. That teaching is at the very heart and core of the Old Testament. It is every whit as much at the heart and core of the New Testament. The New Testament is just as much opposed as the Old Testament is to the thought that there are more Gods than one. Yet the New Testament with equal clearness teaches that the Father is God and the Son is God and the Holy Spirit is God, and that these three are not three aspects of the same person but three persons standing in a truly personal relationship to one another. There we have the great doctrine of the three persons but one God.

That doctrine is a mystery. No human mind can fathom it. Yet what a blessed mystery it is! The Christian's heart melts within him in gratitude and joy when he thinks of the divine love and condescension that has thus lifted the veil and allowed us sinful creatures a look into the very depths of the being of God.

XI

WHAT IS THE DEITY OF CHRIST?

WE have been talking about the great mystery of the Trinity. We have seen that according to the Bible there is but one God but that that one God is in three persons, the Father, the Son and the Holy Ghost. There are some places in the New Testament where all three persons of the Godhead are mentioned in the same verse. But much the more important or extensive part of the Biblical proof of the doctrine of the Trinity is found in those passages where parts of the great doctrine are so mentioned as that when they are put together the completed doctrine inevitably appears. I want to begin to talk to you today about one great central part of the doctrine. I want to talk to you about the deity of our Lord Jesus Christ.

But before I can say a single word to you about the deity of Christ, I must tell you what that term "the deity of Christ" means, or rather I must make perfectly clear to you what it does not mean. I must make perfectly clear to you the fact that the term "deity of Christ" and the assertion "Jesus is God" are often so employed today as to mean something quite contrary to the Bible and to the Christian faith.

Do you not see, my friends, that when a man says he believes in the deity of Christ, or when he says he believes that Jesus is God, the significance of such assertions depends altogether upon the question what the man who makes them means by the term "deity" or the term "God."

If a man has a low view of deity, then, when he says that he believes in the deity of Christ, that means that he has a low view of Christ; and if he has a low view of God, then, when he says that he believes that Jesus is God, that means that he has a low view of Jesus.

But here is where the confusion comes in. A Christian man, hearing some unbeliever say that he believes in the deity of Christ or believes that Jesus is God, attributes to that unbeliever the *Christian* definition of the term "deity" or the term "God." He simply assumes that the term "deity" or the term "God" means what Christians have always taken those terms as meaning. That is, he assumes that those terms refer to a personal God, Creator and Ruler of the world, separate by a mighty gulf from all finite things. The consequence is that he is very much impressed when those terms are used about Jesus by a man who otherwise seemed to be very far from the Christian faith. "Did you not hear that man say," he exclaims, "that he believes in the deity of Christ; did you not hear him call Jesus 'God'? Well, if he believes in the deity of Christ, if he is willing to call Jesus 'God,' he cannot be so very wrong. He may be unorthodox in some particulars, but surely the root of the matter must be in him."

When I hear Christian people talking in that fashion about one of the noted unbelievers of the day, I have the sad feeling that those Christian people are, if I may use plain language, being deceived.

I am not a bit ashamed of laying stress upon this point, because I think it is a matter of profound importance. If I were sure I could get it really straight in your minds I should think it worth while to devote not merely a part of one lecture to it, but a whole series of lectures. The more I look out upon the condition of the Church, the more I am convinced that untold harm is being done by this double use of the term "deity" and of the term "God." The willingness of unbelievers to use the terms in *their* sense, coupled with the proneness of Christians to understand them in theirs, is causing the great issue in the Church between Christianity and unbelief to be obscured. What is the result? The result is that the Church is being undermined from within. Christian people are being lulled to sleep by this use of orthodox terminology. Unbelievers are quietly gaining control. The young people of the Church are being trained up in unbelief. Precious souls are being destroyed.

What ought we to do in such a situation? I will tell you what we ought to do, my friends. We ought to seek light, and we ought to pray God for light. We ought to pray God that people may cease to be satisfied by a word, but may insist on looking at the meaning of the word.

Now the Christian meaning of the term "deity of Christ" is fairly clear. The Christian believes that there is a personal God, Creator and Ruler of the universe, a God who is infinite, eternal and unchangeable. So when the Christian says that Jesus Christ is God, or when he says that he believes in the deity of Christ, he means that that same person who is known to history as Jesus of Nazareth existed, before He became man, from all eternity as infinite, eternal and unchangeable God, the second person of the holy Trinity.

Very different is the use of the term "deity of Christ" or the term "God," as it is applied to Jesus by many leaders in the modern Church.

You can tell that they are using the term in some sense entirely different from the Christian sense because of the things that they say about Jesus in detail, or, even more, because of the things that they will *not* say. They will not say that Jesus was born of a virgin. They will not say that He worked miracles. They will not say that the things that He said were always true; they will not say that He died as our substitute on the cross; they will not say that He rose from the tomb on the third day. Yet, they say, He was God.

When they say He was God, are they saying something orthodox? Is that orthodox assertion of theirs to be put to their credit over against the unorthodox assertions that they have made?

We answer: "No, a thousand times no!" When these men say that they believe in the deity of Christ or that they believe Jesus is God, that is not the most orthodox but the least orthodox thing that they say. It is an orthodox and a blessed thing to say that the Jesus of the Bible is God; but to say that this poor deluded enthusiast of modern reconstruction is God is horrible blasphemy. How low these men must think of God if they can use His name in that way!

But in what sense do these men use the term "God" or the term "deity" when they apply it to the purely human Jesus—their purely human Jesus whom they have reconstructed after their rejection of the New Testament account?

Sometimes they mean by calling Jesus God merely that they try to enter into the same religious experience as the religious experience of those who in past generations called Jesus God. In the creeds of the Church, they say, Jesus is called God. We do not believe, they say, that He is God in the sense in which the authors of those creeds believed it. Shall we then cease to use the creeds? Not at all, they say. When the authors of the creeds called Jesus God, they were expressing in the language of their day a very precious experience which we also can share. So, they say, we can use the creeds still. We do not, of course, take them literally. But we can use them as expressions of the historic faith of the Church. We can still hold to the underlying spiritual meaning of the doctrines that they contain—including the doctrine of the deity of Christ.

Such repetitions of the creeds and such professions of belief in the deity of Christ are doing untold harm in the Church today. No doubt they are comforting to the men who practise them. I have sympathy with those men. To those men this use of traditional terminology seems like the stained glass in an old cathedral. It puts everything in a sort of dim religious light; it seems to impart a solemn glow of sanctity to what would appear to be bald unbelief if it were viewed in the cruel light of day.

But the trouble is that ordinary people in the Church are being deceived. They hear a man repeating the creeds. He seems to be repeating them with the utmost fervor. He is particularly fervent in expressing his belief in the deity of Christ. They simply assume that he means by the deity of Christ what people have always meant by it. So they tolerate him in the Church and put him in a position of authority. Time goes on. Many such men are put into positions of greater and greater authority. They undermine the faith of the Church, partly by their words, but more particularly by their silence. A deadly vagueness gradually affects the Church's witness. The young people of the Church are not soundly indoctrinated. People do not know what is wrong, but the Church loses its power. Finally, the mask is thrown off. The people who really believe in the Bible and in the creed of the Church and who are dead in earnest about that belief are treated as trouble-makers. The Church sinks down into a merger with the world.

That has been the process in many Churches of our day. But it is not in that way that we believe in the deity of Christ. When we say we believe in the deity of Christ, when we repeat the great creeds, we are not just using a form of words that meant something to somebody of long ago. No, we are saying something that we do honestly hold ourselves to be true. We are not just giving expression to the historic faith of the Church, but we are giving expression to *our* faith. We are saying that the historic faith of the Church is what we ourselves believe.

But aside from a merely traditional use of ancient terms, what is the actual meaning attributed to the terms "deity" and "God" by those who have given up the meaning that is found in the Bible and in the great creeds of the Church? What do modern unbelievers mean by speaking of the "deity of Christ" and what do they mean by calling Jesus "God"?

I think a twofold answer will have to be given to that question. Unbelievers who use the term "deity of Christ" and the term "God" as applied to Jesus mean usually one or the other of two things by those terms.

In the first place, some of them use the terms in what may be called a pantheizing sense. That is, they are willing to call Jesus God because they hold that all of us are God. They put only a difference of degree and not a difference of kind between Jesus' deity and ours. God, they say, is not a far-off God. His life pulsates through the life of all the world. He has always been incarnating Himself in men and women. At one point He incarnated Himself with particular fulness—namely, in Jesus of Nazareth. But that incarnation was not different in kind from the incarnation in other men. It was different in degree but not in kind. What is revealed by the appearance of such a man as Jesus on the earth is that God and man are essentially one.

It is needless to say that that view of the deity of Christ is just about the diametrical opposite of the Christian view, which the Bible teaches. According to the Bible, what is revealed by the appearance of Jesus upon the earth is not that God and man are one, but rather that God and man are not one. God is God and man is man. There can be no confusion between the two. Moreover, man is separate from God by the awful abyss of sin. Hence—just because of that separation between God and man—the eternal Son of God, Second Person of the holy Trinity, took upon Himself our nature, by an act that was done not many

times but once and once only, and so because of that
one act "was, and continueth to be God, and man, in
two distinct natures, and one person, for ever."

I am not going to try to speak today of the relation
between the divine nature and the human nature in the
person of Christ. That belongs to a later talk in this
series, or rather to a talk in some subsequent series.
But what I want now to do is simply to say that the
words, "Jesus is God," have no real meaning, certainly
no Biblical or Christian meaning, unless they go with
the supplementary belief that *we* most emphatically
are *not* God.

In the second place, other unbelievers use the terms
"deity of Christ" or the term "God" as applied to
Jesus in what may be called an anti-metaphysical or
positivistic sense. I trust you have some spirit left in
you when I use words as long as those. I do not expect
all of you to understand that word "positivistic" right
at the start, but I do hope to make you understand the
thing that I mean by that word. I mean to designate
by it the view of people who regard the human life of
the man Jesus as the only God that they know. People
used to believe, they say, that there is a personal God,
Creator and Ruler of the world. But we no longer
believe that—at least we are quite uncertain about it.
It belongs to the realm of metaphysics, which is a very
doubtful realm. The only things that we can be really
certain about are the things that we can see and hear,

the things that are found here in this world in which we live. So if we are to have a God, a modern God, we must find Him here in the midst of us—here in this plainly visible realm.

Now we want to find a God, say the men of this way of thinking. People who used to believe in that old metaphysical God, Maker and Ruler of the universe, had something that we are in danger of losing. They had religion. They had a Being who could call forth ennobling emotions of reverence and awe. We need those emotions. We need something to call them forth. We need something to worship.

Where shall we find something to call forth these emotions? Where shall we find something to worship? Where shall we find an adequate object of religious devotion to take the place of that personal Creator in whom we no longer believe? We must find it here upon this earth, say these people of whom we are now speaking. Where then shall we find it?

Why, we find it, they say, in the life of a certain man named Jesus. He was not of course the Creator of the world. He was a man like the rest of men. But His moral life can call forth the same reverence as past generations used to give to the supposed Creator of the world. So although metaphysics is gone religion remains. Men used to have the ennobling emotion of reverence as they turned to the starry heavens and said: "The heavens declare the glory of God; and the firma-ment sheweth his handywork " We no longer believe all that. But we can experience those same ennobling emotions by contemplating the human life of the man Jesus.

Such is a very common view of what men call "the deity of Christ." What shall we say about that view? What shall we say about that way of worshiping Jesus? I will tell you what I think we ought to say about it. I think we ought to say about it that it is a terrible sin.

Please do not misunderstand me. It is not a sin to worship Jesus. On the contrary, it is the highest and noblest privilege and duty ever given to man. It is not a sin to worship the real Jesus. It is not a sin to worship the Jesus who is God and man. But it is a sin to manufacture a Jesus who was man only and not God, and then after you have manufactured that purely human Jesus to bow down and worship Him.

Do you not see what that kind of worship of the moral life of a supposedly purely human Jesus, a Jesus who is regarded merely as the ideal man—do you not see what that worship of such a purely human Jesus really means? It means that the man who engages in it has committed the ancient and terrible sin of worshiping humanity. It means that he has worshiped and served the creature rather than the Creator, and that is a sin indeed.

The upshot of what I have been saying is this—that when men today say that Christ is God they often do so not because they think high of Christ but because they think desperately low of God.

That is not at all the way in which the Bible says that Christ is God. When the Bible says that Christ is God, it does not do that by dragging God down. It does not ask us to forget a single thing that it has said about the stupendous majesty of God. No, it asks us to remember every one of those things in order that we may apply them all to Jesus Christ.

The Bible tells us in the first verse that God in the beginning created the heaven and the earth. Does it ask us to forget that when it tells us that Jesus Christ is God? No, it asks us to remember that. It says of Jesus Christ: "All things were made by him; and without him was not anything made that was made."

The Bible tells us that God is infinite, eternal, and unchangeable. Does it ask us to forget that when it tells us that Christ is God? No, it tells us to remember that. "I am Alpha and Omega," says Christ, "the beginning and the end, the first and the last." "Before Abraham was, I am." "In the beginning was the Word." "He is before all things, and by him all things consist."

The Bible tells us that God is holy. Does it ask us to forget that when it tells us that Christ is God? Let the whole New Testament give the answer.

The Bible tells us that God is mysterious. Does it ask us to forget that when it tells us that Christ is God? No, it tells us that there are mysteries in Christ which only God can know No one knoweth the Son but the Father, says Jesus, as no one knoweth the Father but the Son.

The Bible tells us that God is the final judge. Does it ask us to forget that when it tells us that Jesus is God? No, Jesus Himself said, in the Sermon on the Mount, that He would sit upon the judgment throne to judge all the earth.

Everywhere it is the same, my friends. The Bible from Genesis to Revelation presents a stupendous view of God, and then it tells us that Jesus Christ is all that God is.

What interest has the Christian man in all that? What interest has the Christian man in knowing that Jesus Christ is very God, what interest in knowing that it was through Him that the worlds were made, what interest in knowing that He pervades the remotest bounds, what interest in knowing that He is infinite in knowledge and in power?

No interest, say modern unbelievers; these things are mere metaphysics.

Every interest, say Christians; these things are the very breath of our lives.

We have trusted in Jesus. But how far can we trust Him? Just in this transitory life? Just in this little speck that we call the earth? If we can trust Him only thus far we are of all men most miserable. We are surrounded by stupendous forces; we are surrounded by the immensity of the unknown. After our little span of life there is a shelving brink with the infinite beyond. And still we are subject to fear—not only fear of destruction but a more dreadful fear of meeting with the infinite and holy God.

So we should be if we had but a human Christ. But now is Christ our Saviour, the one who says, "Thy sins are forgiven thee," revealed as very God. And we believe. Such a faith is a mystery to us who possess it; it seems folly to those who have it not. But if possessed it delivers us forever from fear. The world to us is all unknown; it is engulfed in an ocean of infinity. But it contains no mysteries to our Saviour. He is on the throne. He pervades the remotest bounds. He inhabits infinity. With such a Saviour we are safe.

XII

DOES THE BIBLE TEACH THE
DEITY OF CHRIST?

In the last talk I began to speak about the deity of
Christ. But I had to point out the disconcerting fact
that in contemporary parlance the term "deity of
Christ" and the term "God" as applied to Jesus mean
practically nothing. They are used in so many different
senses that the use of these terms has in itself lost all
significance. Unbelievers who have a very low view of
Jesus indeed are perfectly willing to say that Jesus is
God. They are willing to say that Jesus is God not
because they have a high view of Jesus but because
they have a low view of God.

It is a relief to turn from such intellectual quagmires,
where words no longer mean what they say, to the
Bible. In modern parlance, with its boundless degrada-
tion of formerly lofty terms, there is no solid footing;
but it is not so in the Bible. The Bible defines its terms
with the utmost clearness, and therefore when the Bible
says that Jesus is God, we readers of the Bible know
exactly where we stand.

Just now, therefore, we have a much pleasanter task

than that which we had in the last talk. We are going to try to begin to set forth in positive fashion a little bit at least of what the Bible says about the deity of Christ.

If we were going to do so with any completeness we should have to begin with the Old Testament. It is true, the Old Testament does not set forth the doctrine of the deity of Christ with any fulness. I do not suppose that either the prophets or their hearers knew in any clear fashion that the coming Messiah was to be one of the persons in the Godhead. Yet there are wonderful intimations of the doctrine of the deity of Christ even in the Old Testament. The outstanding fact is that the hope of a coming Messiah, as it appears with increasing clearness in the Old Testament books, goes far beyond any mere expectation of an earthly king of David's line. The Messiah, according to the Old Testament, is clearly to be a supernatural person, and he is clearly possessed of attributes that are truly divine.

It has often been observed that before the time of Christ, there were two types of Messianic expectation among the Jews. According to one type, the Messiah was to be a king of David's line; according to the other, He was to be a heavenly being suddenly appearing in the clouds of heaven to judge the world.

Both of these types of later Jewish expectation are rooted in the Old Testament. The Old Testament represents the Messiah both as a king of David's line and also as a supernatural person to appear with the clouds of heaven. The former of these two representations appears, for example, in the seventh chapter of II Samuel, where a never-ending line of kings to be descended from David is promised; and it appears even more clearly in the passages where the coming of one supreme king of David's line is promised. The latter of the two representations appears, for example, in the seventh chapter of Daniel, where a mysterious person "like unto a son of man" is seen, in the prophet's vision, in the presence of the "ancient of days"—a mysterious person to whom is given a universal and everlasting dominion.

These two types of Messianic expectation in the Old Testament are by no means sharply distinguished from one another. When we examine closely the expected king of David's line, we find that He is to be far more than an ordinary earthly king; we find that He has distinctly supernatural attributes: and, on the other hand, the supernatural figure of the seventh chapter of Daniel is by no means separate from Israel but appears as the representative of the Old Testament people of God.

This possession of both divine and human attributes by the Messiah appears with particular clearness in the ninth chapter of Isaiah. There the coming deliverer is spoken of as one who shall sit upon the throne of David. Yet his kingdom is to be everlasting, and He

Himself is actually called "The Mighty God, The ever-lasting Father, The Prince of Peace." There we have the deity of the coming Messiah presented in the Old Testament in so many words.

Now the glorious thing is that in the New Testament we find these two types of Old Testament promise about the Messiah united, in the fulfilment, in the same Person. How is it that one Person can on the one hand be a man, a king of David's line, and at the same time be the mighty God? The question is not fully answered in the Old Testament. But the New Testament answers it most wonderfully in the great central doctrine of the two natures in the one person of our Lord. Yes, the coming deliverer was indeed to be both Mighty God and a king of David's line, because the Mighty God in strange condescension and love became man for our sakes "and so was, and continueth to be God, and man, in two distinct natures, and one person, forever."

But we are not now speaking about the relation between the divine nature and the human nature in Christ. What we are now interested in saying is that the Old Testament does teach the deity of the coming Messiah. Here, as at so many other points, there is a wonderful continuity between the Old Testament and the New.

That continuity is fully recognized by the New Testament. The New Testament does not present the doctrine of the Trinity, including the doctrine of the deity of Christ, as though it meant the introduction of a new idea of God. On the contrary, it presents it as being a revelation of the same God as the God who had revealed Himself to Israel in Old Testament times. That is finely brought out in the article on the Trinity by B. B. Warfield, to which we have already referred.[1] The Jehovah of the Old Testament is presented in the New Testament as being a triune God; but He is the same God throughout both the Old Testament and the New.

Hence it is only what is to be expected when we find that the New Testament applies to Christ Old Testament passages where the God of Israel is called by His holiest and most precious name, "Jehovah." Could there be any clearer testimony to the full deity of Jesus Christ?

Dr. Warfield rightly calls attention also to the matter-of-course way in which this identity of the triune God of the New Testament with the covenant God of Israel appears in the New Testament books. The New Testament writers are apparently not conscious of saying anything revolutionary. They assume the doctrine of the deity of Christ more than they expressly teach it. Why do they assume it? Dr. Warfield gives the answer.[2] They assume it because it had already been

[1] Warfield, *Biblical Doctrines,* 1929, pp. 142 f.
[2] Warfield, *op. cit.,* pp. 143-147.

established by the fact of the coming of the Son of God in the flesh. The doctrine was established by the fact of the incarnation before it was set forth in words. When the eternal Son of God became man in order to redeem sinners on the cross, and when the Holy Spirit was sent to apply that redeeming work of the Son of God to those who should be saved, then the doctrine of the Trinity was made known to men. The Church from the very beginning was founded upon that doctrine; it was the factual revelation of that doctrine by the coming of the Son and the coming of the Spirit that ushered in the new dispensation.

However, although it was the factual revelation of the doctrine which in a true sense came first, yet the doctrine is taught also in words, and taught in the plainest possible way. In setting forth the way in which it is taught, one great difficulty is the difficulty of selection. The whole New Testament teaches the deity of Christ, and that is what makes it hard for us to decide what individual passages we shall mention. Where the store is so very rich, it is hard to make a selection from it.

Let us begin with the point of time at which the New Testament narrative begins. Let us begin with the annunciation of the birth of John the Baptist, as it is recorded in the first chapter of Luke. The angel promises to Zacharias that he will have a son, who will, in accordance with the prophecy in Malachi, go before the Lord to make ready His people for Him.[3] There is here no clear reference to the Messiah as a distinct person. The promised son of Zacharias is to go before Jehovah, or, in the Greek form, "the Lord"; but it is not said that he is to go before the Messiah. Yet there is no doubt but that the author of the Gospel according to Luke, when he quotes the angel's words, identifies that coming of Jehovah with which the Malachi prophecy dealt and to which the angel alludes with the coming of Jesus Christ. The coming of Jehovah is the coming of Christ. There is also no doubt but that in making that identification the author of this gospel is in accordance with the whole New Testament and in accordance with the real meaning of what the angel said. We have here just one instance of that stupendous fact of which we have already spoken—the fact that the New Testament writers apply to Jesus things that the Old Testament says of Jehovah. The whole New Testament is based upon the thought that there is some strange essential unity between Jesus Christ and the covenant God of Israel.

Then we have the annunciation of the angel to the virgin Mary.[4] The annunciation is partly in Old Testament terms. Mary's son is to sit on the throne of David; and when it is said that of His kingdom there is to be no end, that also does not go beyond what the Old Testament had promised about the Messiah. But then

[3] Lk. 1:16 f.   [4] Lk. 1:30-38.

a great mystery is revealed. The promised child is not to have a human father by ordinary generation, but is to be conceived by the Holy Ghost in the womb of a virgin mother. Even that—at least the part of it that sets forth the fact that the mother is to be a virgin—is found in Old Testament prophecy (in Isa. 7:14)—but that prophecy had not been understood among the Jews. Now, just before the fulfilment, the prophecy is repeated in fuller and more glorious terms. The conception of this child in the womb of the virgin Mary is to be a miracle wrought by the immediate power of the Spirit of God. That miracle is one of the things that will show the child to be rightly called "holy" and "Son of God."

Evidently the term "Son of God" is here used in some very lofty sense. It does not designate the promised child merely as the Messiah, though sometimes the Messiah was called "Son of God." Evidently the term is used here in some unique and stupendous sense.

At twelve years of age, the child Jesus was found in the Temple. Joseph and Mary had sought Him sorrowing, and at last they found Him among the doctors, hearing them and asking them questions. "Son," they said, "why hast thou thus dealt with us? behold, thy father and I have sought thee sorrowing." Then came the strange answer of the boy Jesus: "Wist ye not that I must be about my Father's business?" [5] When Mary

[5] Lk. 2:48 f.

spoke of the father of that twelve-year-old boy, she meant his human father, the one who stood to him in a relation more like that of a father than did any other human being. When the boy Jesus spoke of His Father in reply, He meant God. Notice that He did not say "Our Father" when He spoke of God. No, He said "My Father." He was Son of God in a sense entirely different from that which would apply to any other person who ever lived upon this earth.

That brings us to one of the strangest things about the way in which Jesus all through the Gospels speaks of God. This strange thing appears not only in the Gospel according to John, which modern unbelief rejects so radically as untrue, but also in the Synoptic Gospels. The strange thing is that Jesus according to all four of the Gospels never speaks of God as "our Father," classing Himself with His disciples in that word "our." He says "My Father" and He says to His disciples "Your Father," but never does He say "Our Father" classing Himself with His disciples in that filial relationship to God. The Lord's prayer begins with those words "Our Father," but Jesus certainly did not pray that prayer with His disciples, because that prayer contains a confession of sin, and Jesus never had any sin to confess. It was a prayer that He taught His disciples, not a prayer that He prayed Himself. The significant fact remains, therefore. Jesus never appears in the Gospels as saying "Our Father" to God together with His disciples. God was His Father, and God was their Father; but He was His Father in an entirely different sense from the sense in which He was their Father. Jesus was Son of God in an entirely unique way.

At the beginning of the Gospel according to Mark, with the parallel passages in Matthew and Luke, we are told about the beginning of Jesus' public ministry. That event was marked by a miracle. The Spirit descended upon Jesus, and there was a voice from heaven that said: "Thou art my beloved Son, in thee I am well pleased." [6] It is possible that the good pleasure of God which is here spoken of is the definite act of approval accomplished at the moment when Jesus was sent forth into His public ministry. Yet, even so, that divine act of approval is evidently regarded as rooted in a unique relationship in which the Person thus approved had always stood toward God. Jesus did not become Son of God because He had divine approval, but He had that divine approval because He had always been Son of God.

For a further discussion of that question and similar questions I may refer you incidentally to the learned and most illuminating book on "The Self-Disclosure of Jesus" by Geerhardus Vos.[7]

At any rate Jesus now comes forward in His public

[6] Mk. 1:11.
[7] Vos, *The Self-Disclosure of Jesus* (1926), especially pp. 185-188.

ministry. In what light does He present Himself in that public ministry?

Here one great central fact stares us in the face. I think it would hardly be possible to lay too much stress upon it. It is this—that Jesus does not present Himself merely as an example for faith but presents Himself as the object of faith. That fact appears not merely in the Gospel according to John, which unbelievers reject as altogether unhistorical; but it appears also in the three Synoptic Gospels, and in the Synoptic Gospels it appears even in those parts which are supposed by modern criticism, rightly or wrongly, to come from the earliest sources underlying the Gospels. You cannot get away from it anywhere in the Gospels. It is all-pervasive. That fact has been demonstrated in particularly convincing fashion by James Denney in his book "Jesus and the Gospel." I do not commend that book to you in general. In some respects it is a sadly mistaken book. But it does show in a singularly convincing way that everywhere in the New Testament, including the Synoptic Gospels, and including the sources supposed rightly or wrongly to underlie the Synoptic Gospels, Jesus is represented not as a mere example for faith but as the object of faith.

What do we mean by saying that? What do we mean by saying that Jesus is presented not primarily as an example for faith but as the object of faith? We mean something very simple and at the same time something very stupendous. We mean that Jesus did not come forward merely saying: "Look at me; I am practising the true religion, and I bid you practise the same religion as that which I am practising." We mean that He did not come forward merely saying: "Look at me; I have faith in God, and I bid you have faith in God like my faith in God." We mean that He did not come forward merely saying: "Look at me; I regard God as my Father, and I bid you to regard God as your Father too in the same sense as that in which I regard Him as my Father."

It is so that modern unbelievers represent Jesus. They regard Him as a guide out into a larger type of religious life. They regard Him as being the founder of Christianity because He was the first Christian. They regard Christianity as consisting in imitation of the religious life of Jesus. So they love to speak of "the religion of Jesus"; they love to speak of the gospel *of* Jesus in distinction from a gospel *about* Jesus. Thus they degrade Jesus to the position of a mere teacher and example. They turn away from the gospel that has Him as its substance to a gospel which was merely the gospel that He preached.

When they do that, it is evident that they are turning away from what has been known as Christianity for the past nineteen hundred years. But they are also turning away from Jesus Himself as He is presented to us in all the sources of historical information that we know anything about. According to all the four Gospels, and according to all the supposed sources which modern criticism has tried to detect back of the four Gospels, Jesus put Himself into His gospel; the gospel *of* Jesus was also a gospel *about* Jesus; the gospel that He preached was also a gospel that offered Him as Saviour. He did not say merely: "Have faith in God like the faith that I have in God," but He said: "Have faith *in me.*"

That appears of course with the utmost clearness in the Gospel according to John. But it also appears in the Synoptic Gospels. There was, indeed, according to the Synoptic Gospels, a period in the public ministry of Jesus when He did not ordinarily make His own person the express subject of systematic discourse. But if you look a little deeper, you see that everywhere Jesus was offering Himself as the Saviour of men and was asking them to have faith in Him.

That appears, for example, in His miracles of healing. "Thy faith hath saved thee," He says; "go in peace." Well, faith in whom? Perhaps we might be tempted to say merely, "Faith in God like the faith which Jesus had in God." But I bid you read the narratives with care and ask yourselves whether that interpretation really does justice to them. I think you will find that it does not. No, Jesus was presenting Himself when He worked those miracles as one in whom He was bidding men have confidence. No doubt He was bidding them have confidence in God the Father. But the point is that that confidence in God the Father was also confidence in Him. The faith that saved those people was faith in Jesus Christ.

He was saving those people from bodily ills, but He was also saving their souls from sin. That becomes explicit in the healing of the paralytic borne of four, where Jesus says not only "Arise and walk" but "Thy sins are forgiven thee." But it is really implied in the cases where it is not expressed. Jesus according to all the Gospels saves men from sin, and the means which He uses to save them from sin is the faith which He bids them have in Him the Saviour.

Thus Jesus, according to all the Gospels, presents Himself as the object of a truly religious faith. Well, who is the object of a truly religious faith? The answer is very simple. He is God. The way in which, in all the Gospels and even in the sources supposed, rightly or wrongly, to underlie the Gospels, Jesus presents Himself as the object of faith is a tremendous testimony by Jesus Himself to His own deity. That testimony does not appear merely in individual passages. It is a kind of atmosphere that pervades the whole picture, or, to change the figure, a foundation that sustains the whole building. If you ignore it, the whole account which the Bible gives of Jesus becomes a hopeless puzzle.

In the next talk, I want to **continue** to **deal** with

the deity of Christ. Today I have been able to do no more than make a beginning in the presentation of that great subject. I wonder what you think about it. What do you think of Jesus Christ? Do you think of Him, with modern unbelievers, merely as the initiator of a higher type of religious life, the discoverer of certain permanent facts about the Fatherhood of God and the brotherhood of man? Or do you think of Him, as Christians do, as the Lord of Glory, the eternal Son of God become man to save you from your sins? Or, finally, are you undecided with regard to Him? Are you undecided which of these two views you will hold? Do you belong to that great army of persons who stand outside the household of faith and look longingly at the warmth and joy within? Are you hindered from entering in by gloomy doubts? If you belong to that third class, we pray God that you may be led to say at least: "Lord, I believe; help thou mine unbelief." If you do say that, the Lord will help your unbelief, as He helped the man who said that so long ago, and will bring you into the clear shining of faith.

XIII

THE SERMON ON THE MOUNT AND THE
DEITY OF CHRIST

WE are now in the midst of our discussion of the great theme, the deity of Jesus Christ. Was Jesus a mere man, a leader into a higher and better type of religious experience, or was He the eternal Son of God become man to save us from the guilt and power of sin?

We have already begun to point out what the Bible says about this question. In particular, we have pointed out that all four of the Gospels, and even the sources supposed, rightly or wrongly, to underlie the Gospels, represent Jesus not merely as an example of faith but as the object of faith—that is, they represent Jesus not as saying merely, "Have faith in God like the faith which I have in God," but as saying, "Have faith in me." But that means that the four Gospels teach the deity of Christ and represent Jesus Himself as teaching it. The object of a truly religious faith is none other than God.

I want now to show you how extraordinarily pervasive in the Gospels is the lofty view of Jesus Christ which necessarily goes with His offer of Himself as the object of faith. People try to escape from that lofty view of Christ. They like to regard Jesus just as a teacher and example; they say that this whole notion about His deity is an unfortunate metaphysical notion that has nothing to do with vital religion. Let us get away from metaphysics and theology, they say, and, instead, just get up and obey Jesus' commands; if we obey His commands we are honoring Him more than we could honor Him by any amount of intellectual convictions regarding His deity.

Well, my friend, I will say to a man of this way of thinking, where will you turn in the Gospels to get away from a lofty view of the person of Christ; where will you turn to find a Jesus who simply gave men directions for the ordering of their lives and did not demand that they should have any particular view about Him? Here is a New Testament, my friend; will you just open it anywhere you like in order to prove your point.

I suppose that if I should say that to one of the advocates of this non-doctrinal Christianity, he would be most apt to turn, among all the passages in the New Testament, to the Sermon on the Mount.[1] In the Sermon on the Mount, it is often said, we have a program for Christian living that is quite independent of the niceties of orthodox theology, and if we should just be willing to live that kind of life it would be a great deal better than disputing about theological questions or

[1] Matt., chapters 5-7.

even being too anxious to get a completely orthodox notion about Jesus Himself.

Well, my friend, you have turned to the Sermon on the Mount. I did not choose it. You chose it. It is your favorite passage. You cannot object therefore if we examine it a little for ourselves to see whether it really teaches that kind of non-doctrinal religion that you so enthusiastically advocate. In particular, you cannot object if we examine it to see whether it is really silent about those stupendous claims of Jesus which so trouble you in other parts of the New Testament.

All right, then; we are going to put preconceived opinions aside and examine the Sermon on the Mount for ourselves.

What happens to us when we do that? I will tell you very plainly. We find that the Sermon on the Mount teaches and presupposes that same stupendous view of Jesus Christ which underlies all the rest of the Gospels.

The Sermon on the Mount might seem to begin in a way unfavorable to that view and favorable to the advocate of a non-doctrinal Christianity who is not interested in the question what sort of person Jesus is. It begins with the Beatitudes, and the Beatitudes might seem at first sight to be independent of any particular view regarding the one who spoke them. "Blessed are the poor in spirit: for theirs is the kingdom of heaven" —does not that remain true whatever we think of the person who uttered it?

Well, I am not sure even about that. I am not sure but that in all of the Beatitudes we detect a strange note of authority which would be overwrought and pathological in any other person than the Jesus of the Bible. Who is this who tells with such extraordinary assurance what sort of persons will be in the kingdom of God? Who is this that announces to men rewards that only God can give?

But let that pass for the moment. The thing that is clear is that Jesus does not finish the Beatitudes before He comes to speak in the most stupendous way about Himself. What is the last of the Beatitudes? Is it merely a blessing pronounced upon people who possess a certain quality of soul? Not at all. It is a blessing pronounced upon people who stand in a certain relation to Jesus Himself. Here is what it is: "Blessed are ye, when men shall revile you, and persecute you, and shall say all manner of evil against you falsely, for my sake." Notice those words "for my sake." They contain a tremendous claim on the part of Jesus. Men are to be willing to bear His name, and if they are not ashamed to bear His name they are to stand in the final judgment. Imagine any mere man saying that! Imagine anyone other than Jesus saying: "Blessed are ye if ye suffer on account of me." We have here the words of the same Jesus as was the One who said: "If any man come to me, and hate not his father, and mother, and **wife, and children, and brethren, and sisters, yea, and** his own life also, he cannot be my disciple," [2] the same Jesus as the One who said: "Whosoever therefore shall be ashamed of me and of my words in this adulterous and sinful generation; of him also shall the Son of man be ashamed, when he cometh in the glory of his Father with the holy angels." [3] Who can claim such an exclusive devotion as that—a devotion which shall take precedence of even the holiest of earthly ties, a devotion upon which a man's eternal destiny depends? God can, but can any mere man?

Then comes that great section of the Sermon on the Mount where Jesus declares Himself to have come not to destroy the law or the prophets but to fulfil. "Ye have heard that it was said to the men of old time," He says, and then makes several quotations. Those quotations contain in part sentences found in the Old Testament. Over against those quotations, Jesus in every case puts something of His own: "Ye have heard that it was said . . . but I say unto you." No doubt it may be held that Jesus in none of these instances is setting what He says over against what the Old Testament says, but in every instance is merely setting what He says over against what the Jewish teachers had wrongly held that the Old Testament said. But even then the fact remains that what He sets forth against the wrong interpretation of the Old Testament passages is not just a right interpretation but something wonderfully fresh and

[2] Lk. 14:26.   [3] Mk. 8:38.

new. Plainly Jesus puts His own sayings here on a level with the Old Testament pronouncements which He certainly regarded as the very Word of God.

I ask you to consider for a moment that authority with which Jesus speaks, that authority which causes Him to put His own pronouncements fully on a level with the Old Testament pronouncements. What is the nature of that authority which Jesus here claims?

Well, prophets claimed authority. They asked that people should receive what they said as a message from God. Was then the authority which Jesus is here claiming merely the authority of a prophet? No, most emphatically it was not merely that. The prophets spoke with a divine authority. But it was a delegated authority, and it was delegated to them in a temporary way. There were times when the prophets became spokesmen of God, but they were spokesmen of God merely because they became for the moment channels for the Holy Spirit. They were not in general infallible. They had no authority which was granted them as a permanent possession to be used as they saw fit. When they came forward as prophets they were careful to give all honor to God.

Thus the characteristic way in which the prophets introduced their utterances was with the words, "Thus saith the Lord." By that they meant to say: "I am not saying this as my own word, but it is God who *is* saying it; I am merely the mouthpiece of God."

Now unquestionably Jesus was a prophet. Undoubtedly the catechism that I learned in childhood was right when it told me that He was a prophet as well as a priest and a king.

But although Jesus was a prophet, He was also vastly more than a prophet. So He does not introduce these utterances of His in the Sermon on the Mount in the way in which the utterances of a prophet are introduced. He does not say, "Thus saith the Lord." No, He says, "*I* say." He comes forward with His own authority, and that authority He places fully on a level with the authority of God as it was found expressed in the Old Testament.

I am not forgetting the places in the Gospels where the dependence of the man Jesus upon God is set forth. Those passages are found particularly just in the Gospel according to John—just in that Gospel where the deity of Christ is set forth, I will not say more clearly (since it is set forth with the utmost clearness in all the Gospels), but more expressly and fully, than in the other Gospels. Jesus according to the Gospel of John did what He saw God doing, and He said what God told Him to say. All the same, despite this subordination of the man Jesus to God, His authority went far beyond the authority of a prophet. It was an authority which was His own personal right, as belonging to the one who was not merely man but God. You can search all through the words of the prophets and not find anything in the remotest degree resembling that stupendous "I say unto you" of the Sermon on the Mount.

Then I bid you read on to the end of that Sermon on the Mount. "Not every one," says Jesus, "that saith unto me, Lord, Lord, shall enter into the kingdom of heaven; but he that doeth the will of my Father which is in heaven." [*] That is one of the favorite texts of unbelievers. If the whole Sermon on the Mount is their favorite passage, this perhaps, within the Sermon on the Mount, may be regarded as their favorite text.

It is a favorite text with unbelievers not because of its real meaning, but because of the meaning which they wrongly attribute to it. They take it as meaning that if a man is what the world calls a good moral man then he will enter into the Kingdom of God no matter what His attitude toward Jesus may be. But of course that is not what the text says. The text does not say that if a man does the will of God he will enter into the kingdom of God whether He says "Lord, Lord" to Jesus or not. It does not say that any man who does *not* say "Lord, Lord" to Jesus will enter into the kingdom. But what it does say is that even among those who do say "Lord, Lord" to Jesus there are some who will not enter in. Those are the ones who say "Lord, Lord" only with their lips and not with their hearts, and who show that they have not said it with their hearts because they do not say it with their lives.

[*] Matt. 7:21.

However, though for bad reasons, it is a popular text among unbelievers. They ought then to be willing to examine carefully what it says, and we all ought to examine it with them.

When we do examine it, we discover that it involves the most stupendous claim on the part of Jesus. For one thing, it provides an instance of the strange way in which Jesus speaks of God as being His own Father. "Not every one that saith unto me, Lord, Lord, shall enter into the kingdom of heaven," He says, "but he that doeth the will of my Father which is in heaven." "*My* Father," says Jesus, not "*our* Father" or "*the* Father." We spoke of that in the talk just preceding this one. We noticed how it appeared in the answer of the twelve-year-old Jesus in the Temple, and how it runs all through the Gospels. Well, here it is, in the Sermon on the Mount. You cannot get away from it. We do not particularly notice it as we read this verse, because we have become so used to it. But that does not destroy its tremendous significance. Indeed, it vastly increases it. Everywhere Jesus thinks of Himself as being Son of God in some entirely unique sense.

But now let us look at what this verse itself says. We must take it in connection with the following two verses. Those verses also are favorites with the unbelievers of our day. They read as follows:

"Many will say to me in that day, Lord, Lord, have we not prophesied in thy name? and in thy name have cast out devils? and in thy name done many wonderful works?

"And then will I profess unto them, I never knew you: depart from me, ye that work iniquity."

Unbelievers, I suppose, interpret those words as disparaging miracles, and as disparaging the active profession of religion. They interpret them as teaching that if a man leads what the world calls a moral life he does not need to accept any creed or make any definite profession of faith.

That interpretation is of course quite wrong, in the same way as that in which the corresponding interpretation of the preceding verse is wrong. These verses do not say that miracles were unimportant in the apostolic age (when miracles still happened) or that orthodoxy was unimportant then or is unimportant now. They only say that nothing else matters unless a man's heart is changed and unless that change of his heart is shown in a good life. They do not say that orthodoxy is unnecessary or that mighty works in the external world are unimportant, but they only say that orthodoxy without right living is a sham, and that real orthodoxy results in obedience to the commands of God.

But the fact remains that these verses are favorites with unbelievers; they are favorites with those who think that it does not make any difference what a man thinks about God or about Christ and that all that is needed according to Jesus is to live what is ordinarily called a moral life.

All right. Let us just look at these verses so popular among unbelievers. Do they really teach that it does not make any difference what a man thinks about Jesus Christ? I tell you, my friends, the exact reverse is the case. These verses, like all the rest of the New Testament, present a stupendous view of Jesus Christ, and like other sayings of Jesus they present a stupendous claim made by Jesus Himself.

What is the scene to which we are transplanted in these verses? Is it some scene in the course of ordinary history or some scene of merely local or temporary significance? No, it is nothing of the kind. It is the tremendous scene of the last judgment, the court from which there is no appeal, the final decision that determines the eternal destinies of men.

In other words, it is the judgment-seat of God. Well, who is it that is represented here as sitting on the judgment-seat of God; who is it that is represented here in this supposedly pleasant, purely ethical, practical, ultramodern, non-theological Sermon on the Mount, and by this supposedly simple teacher of righteousness who kept His own person out of His message and was careful not to advance any lofty claims—who is it that is represented here in this supposedly purely ethical discourse and by this humble Jesus as sitting one day upon the judgment-seat of God and as determining the eternal destinies of all the world? There can be no doubt whatever about the answer to that question. The one represented here as sitting on the judgment-seat of God is Jesus Himself.

We may not like the answer to that question, but the answer is as plain as plain can be. "Many will say to *me*," Jesus says, "in that day, Lord, Lord . . . and then will *I* profess unto them, I never knew you: depart from me, ye that work iniquity." Who is that "I," and who is that "me"? Is it God the Father? No, it is Jesus; it is the one who speaks these words. Upon Jesus' decision depends the fate of all men. And what is that fate? What is the meaning of that "Depart" which is Jesus' sentence upon those who work iniquity? About this question also there can be no doubt. The Sermon on the Mount itself gives the answer: "And if thy right eye offend thee, pluck it out, and cast it from thee: for it is profitable for thee that one of thy members should perish, and not that thy whole body should be cast into hell." [5] The answer is given also in the whole teaching of Jesus, and it is implied even in the verses with which we now have to do. No, there can be no doubt whatever about what Jesus meant by that word "Depart'"; He meant that those upon whom He would pronounce that sentence to depart would be cast into hell.

The thought of hell as well as the thought of heaven

[5] Matt. 5:29.

runs all through the teaching of Jesus; it gives to His ethical teaching that stupendous earnestness which is its marked characteristic. But how is hell here designated? It is described elsewhere in the Gospels; and never let us forget, whether we call the language "figurative" or not, that it means an eternal and terrible punishment, a punishment of which there is no end. But how is hell designated in this particular passage? The answer may be surprising to some people, but it is perfectly plain. Hell is designated in our passage as being banishment from Jesus.

I do just beg you to think of that for a moment, my friends. Jesus of Nazareth certainly did believe—no good historian can deny it—that He would sit upon the judgment-seat of God at the terrible last judgment day, that His word would be final, and that life in His presence would be heaven and departure from Him would be hell.

What has become of the weak, sentimental, purely human, purely ethical Jesus of modern reconstruction; what has become of your Jesus who was a simple teacher of righteousness and advanced no claim to be God? Have you found your purely human Jesus, and have you escaped from the divine Christ of the creeds, by appealing from the Gospel according to John to the Sermon on the Mount? No, indeed, my friend. The Jesus of the Bible is everywhere exactly the same.

What will you do with that Jesus? Will you treat

Him with a mild approval? Ah, people are so patronizing in the presence of Jesus today. They say such kind, polite things about Him. They are good enough to say that His ethics will solve the problems of society; they are good enough to say that He enunciated some maxims that are better than Jefferson's ten rules and go far beyond Socrates and Confucius and Buddha. They are perfectly ready to let Him influence some departments of their life. They will not receive Him as their Saviour; they are not interested in His atoning blood: but they are so complacent in His presence.

God grant that it may not be so with you, my friends! God grant that you may never treat Jesus with this polite, patronizing approval! God grant that you may not treat Him as a religious genius or as the founder of one of the world's religions! God grant that, instead, you may say to Jesus, with doubting Thomas: "My Lord and my God."

XIV

WHAT JESUS SAID ABOUT HIMSELF

WE have discussed the deity of Christ as it is attested by Jesus Himself in the Sermon on the Mount. We have seen that in the very passage to which unbelievers appeal in support of their view that Jesus kept Himself out of His gospel and merely presented a program of life to be followed first by Him and then by His followers—in that very passage Jesus presents Himself as possessed of an authority that goes far beyond that of any prophet and is in truth an authority that belongs only to God. At the close of our last talk, we were speaking particularly of the passage near the end of the Sermon on the Mount where Jesus presents Himself as the one who is to sit at the last day on the judgment-seat of God and determine the eternal destinies of all the world.

This is by no means the only passage in the Gospels where Jesus so presents Himself as the final judge. Indeed, it is probably because of this thought of Himself as the final judge that He uses one of His favorite titles to designate Himself—namely, the title "the Son of man."

Our first impulse might be to say that the title is a designation of the humanity of Jesus as distinguished from His deity. He was both God and man, and that, we may be tempted to say, is what He meant when He called Himself Son of man as well as Son of God.

If that view of the title were correct, it would certainly be a very lofty title, and it would certainly not be in any contradiction with the deity of Christ. But, as a matter of fact, it is unlikely that the title, "the Son of man," on the lips of Jesus has this meaning at all. It is unlikely that it is intended to designate the humanity of our Lord as distinguished from His deity. It is on the whole unlikely that there is any contrast in the Gospels between the title "Son of man" and the title "Son of God." People who use these titles to designate the two natures of Jesus as both man and God, who call attention, in other words, to the fact that He was both "Son of man" and "Son of God," are probably wrong in their interpretation of the title, right though they unquestionably are in holding that Jesus was both God and man.

The true key to the title, "Son of man," on the lips of our Lord is probably to be found in the seventh chapter of the Book of Daniel, where "one like unto a son of man" appears in the presence of the "ancient of days" and receives an everlasting dominion. When this person is said to be "like unto a son of man," that is not said because He is a man in contrast with God. The contrast is rather with the beasts—lion, bear, leopard, and unnamed beast—that represent the world empires preceding the kingdom of the one like unto a son of man. After the successive appearance of those kingdoms represented by figures designated as being each like the figure of some beast, there arises a Kingdom whose ruler appears in the vision as a man. That Kingdom unlike those other kingdoms is to be everlasting.

This passage in the Book of Daniel had an important influence upon subsequent Messianic expectations among the Jews. In the so-called Ethiopic Book of Enoch, for example,—a book which of course is not in the Bible and does not at all deserve to be there—the title "the Son of man" occurs frequently as the designation of a heavenly personage already existing in heaven but destined to appear in great glory to be the judge of all the world. Now we certainly do not mean for one moment that our Lord made any use of that so-called Book of Enoch. But the thing that *is* likely is that that book does give evidence of the use among the Jews of the great passage in the seventh chapter of Daniel. On the basis of that passage the coming Deliverer had come to be called—in certain Jewish circles at least—"the Son of man," and had come to be thought of as destined to appear with the clouds of heaven and be the judge of all the earth. What our Lord did when He called Himself "the Son of man" was to place the stamp of approval upon this Jewish expectation because it was really in accordance with the Old Testament, and then to apply it to Himself.

It is altogether probable, then, that the title "the Son of man" on the lips of Jesus is distinctly a Messianic title. It does not designate the humanity of Jesus as distinguished from His deity, but it designates Him as being that transcendent, heavenly Person who was to come one day with the clouds of heaven and be the final judge of all the world.

A notable passage in the Book of Acts confirms this view of the title "the Son of man." In Acts 7:55 f., it is said, of the dying martyr Stephen:

"But he, being full of the Holy Ghost, looked up stedfastly into heaven, and saw the glory of God, and Jesus standing on the right hand of God,
"And said, Behold, I see the heavens opened, and the Son of man standing on the right hand of God."

Here the reference to the seventh chapter of Daniel is perfectly plain. Stephen sees essentially the same vision as that which the prophet Daniel had seen; he sees that heavenly figure, the Son of man, appearing in glory in the presence of God.

As Jesus uses the title, the origin of the title is just as clear as it is in the words of the dying Stephen. So, for example, in Mk. 8:38 (with the parallel passages):

"Whosoever therefore shall be ashamed of me and of my words in this adulterous and sinful generation; of him also shall the Son of man be ashamed, when he cometh in the glory of his Father with the holy angels."

So also in Mk. 13:26 (with the parallel passages):

"And then shall they see the Son of man coming in the clouds with great power and glory."

In such passages the reference to the great scene in the seventh chapter of Daniel is perfectly clear.

In other passages, it is true, the reference to that scene is not so direct. Jesus sometimes uses the title, the Son of man, where He is speaking not of His exaltation but of His humiliation. So in Matt. 8:20, where it is said that the "Son of man hath not where to lay his head." So also in the great passage, Mk. 10:45, where Jesus says, regarding His atoning death, that "the Son of man came not to be ministered unto, but to minister, and to give his life a ransom for many." But we may fairly hold that the use of the title in these passages is intended to *contrast* the stupendous dignity properly belonging to the Son of man, the judge and ruler of all the world, with His present humble life. The real pathos of those passages is found in the fact that it was not any ordinary man who had not where to lay His head, and that it was not any ordinary man who came not to be ministered unto but to minister, but the heavenly Son of man, that stupendous figure, who was now more homeless than the foxes and the birds!

Here and there, as Jesus uses the title, there may possibly be a special reference to the humanity of the one so designated, but such passages at the most are rare, and the prevailing significance of the title is that it identifies Jesus with the heavenly Messiah, the stupendous figure spoken of in the seventh chapter of Daniel whose kingdom would be an everlasting kingdom.

That, I may say in passing, is the prevailing opinion today among scholars of widely different shades of opinion, both believers and unbelievers. Here and there a defender of another view of the title appears, but I think it may be said that the prevailing view among careful scholars is what I have just indicated. For a full discussion of this subject I want to refer you to a book to which I have been much indebted—the learned book of Dr. Geerhardus Vos on "The Self-Disclosure of Jesus."

What particularly needs to be said, however, is that whatever view be taken of the origin and meaning of the term, the Son of man, it is at any rate clear that Jesus of Nazareth certainly did claim that He would one day sit on the judgment-seat of God to decide the eternal destinies of men. That claim appears, as we observed very clearly, in the Sermon on the Mount. You cannot get away from it even in the supposedly purely ethical parts of Jesus' teaching. It runs all through the Gospels. Every historian, whether he is a Christian or not, ought to take account of this strange fact—that a certain Jesus, a man who lived in the first century in Palestine, was actually convinced, as He looked out upon the men who thronged about Him, that He would one day sit on the judgment-seat of God and be their judge and the judge and ruler of all the world.

What are you going to do with that claim of Jesus? If you hold it to be true, then Jesus is your King and Lord. If you hold it to be false, then I do not see how in the world you can go on taking Him as a worthy example for your life.

The conviction of Jesus that He would at the last judgment decide the eternal destinies of men was joined with the conviction that He could determine those eternal destinies here and now. He claimed to be able to forgive sins. His opponents got the point of that claim; they got it far better than certain modern persons who trip along so lightly over the things that the Gospels contain. "Why doth this man thus speak?" they said. "He blasphemeth: who can forgive sins but one, even God?" [1] They were right. None can forgive sins but God only. Jesus was a blasphemer if He was a mere man. At that point the enemies saw clear. You may accept the lofty claims of Jesus. You may take Him as very God. Or else you must reject Him as a miserable, deluded enthusiast. There is really no middle ground. Jesus refuses to be pressed into the mould of a mere religious teacher.

Thus we have seen that Jesus' claim of deity runs all through the Gospels. It does not appear merely in this

[1] Mk. 2:7.

passage or that, but is really presupposed in every word that Jesus uttered and in everything that He did.

There was, it is true, a period in His ministry when He did not make His own person for the most part the express subject of His teaching. It was always the background of His teaching and His work; without it everything that He said and did becomes unintelligible. But during a large part of His Galilean ministry, as described by the Synoptic Gospels, He seems not often to have set forth the mystery of His own person in any detailed way.

That lack is wonderfully supplied by the Gospel according to John, which was written by a man who stood in the innermost circle of the disciples of our Lord. But what I want you to observe particularly is that there is no opposition at this point between the Fourth Gospel and the other three. The Christ who is so gloriously set forth in the Gospel according to John is exactly the Christ who is everywhere presupposed in the Synoptic Gospels. Far from being in any contradiction with the Synoptic Gospels, the Gospel according to John, with its rich report of the teaching of our Lord about His own person, provides the key which enables us the better to understand what we are told in Matthew, Mark and Luke.

Here and there, moreover, we have in the Synoptic Gospels just the kind of teaching of our Lord about Himself as that which appears so fully reported by the

Beloved Disciple in the Gospel according to John. That is notably the case with a famous passage in the eleventh chapter of Matthew, which has a close parallel in the tenth chapter of Luke. "All things are delivered unto me of my Father," says Jesus: "and no man knoweth the Son, but the Father; neither knoweth any man the Father, save the Son, and he to whomsoever the Son will reveal him." [*]   Here we have not only the substance of the teaching that appears so fully in the Fourth Gospel but even the form of it. "*The* Father," "*the* Son"—how often those terms appear set over against each other in the Gospel according to John just exactly as they are set over against each other here!

Just consider how wonderfully rich is the content of this verse in its report of the teaching of Jesus about Himself! "No man knoweth the Father but the Son" —that in itself is a very stupendous utterance. It designates Jesus as truly knowing God, and as the only one who knows Him. We think instinctively, as we read, of the words in the Gospel according to John: "No man hath seen God at any time; God only-begotten, which is in the bosom of the Father, he hath declared him." [*] How wonderful is such a knowledge of God! Think of it, my friends. Jesus of Nazareth, a man walking upon this earth, said as He talked to His contemporaries: "No one knoweth God save me." How is such

[*] Matt. 11:27.   [*] John 1:18.

rich knowledge of God possible to any but God Himself?

But that is not all that there is in this saying. No, the saying goes far beyond that. "No one knoweth the Father but the Son"—that is wonderful enough. But that is not all. There is something still more stupendous in this verse. It is this: "No one knoweth the Son but the Father."

Just think what these words mean, my friends. They mean that there are mysteries in the person, Jesus, which none but the infinite and eternal God can know. The two persons, the Father and the Son, are here put in a strange reciprocal relationship. They are both mysterious to all others, but they are known, and fully known, to each other. The Son knows the depths of the Father's being, and the Father knows the depths of the being of the Son. An ineffable mutual knowledge prevails between these two.

What does that mean? It means what is really implied in the Gospels from beginning to end. It means that that strange man who is known to history as Jesus of Nazareth was no mere man, but infinite and eternal and unchangeable God. In this wonderful verse, the twenty-seventh verse of the eleventh chapter of Matthew, we have in summary and in implication the great doctrine of the deity of our Lord, and when we put it together with Jesus' teaching regarding the Holy

Spirit we have the full wonderful teaching of Scripture regarding the three persons in one God.

I have not time in the present talk to speak to you longer about that doctrine; I have not time to set forth further the richness of the Scripture testimony to the deity of our blessed Lord. But there is one thing that I do want to drive home at once.

It is this—that this mysterious verse of which we have just been speaking does not appear as some excrescence in the Gospel picture of Jesus but as an integral part of the whole. When we come upon this "Christological" passage in our reading of the Gospel of Matthew, this passage which has been called "the Johannine passage" because it is so much like the Gospel according to John, do we feel anything like a shock? Do we feel as though we were transplanted into another atmosphere? Do we feel as though we were suddenly dealing with another Christ?

I tell you, my friends, we do not. No, we are dealing with the same Christ as the Christ with whom we have been dealing all through the Gospel according to Matthew; we are dealing with exactly the same Christ as the Christ who spoke, for example, the Sermon on the Mount. We are dealing with the same Christ as the Christ who according to all four Gospels spoke words of solemn warning but also words of an infinite tenderness and grace.

What is the context of this verse with which we have

been dealing in the present talk—this verse which sets forth in such stupendous fashion the majesty of the person of our Lord? Just let me read it to you before we part:

"I thank Thee, O Father, Lord of heaven and earth, because thou hast hid these things from the wise and prudent, and hast revealed them unto babes.

"Even so, Father: for so it seemed good in thy sight."

Then follow the words of which we have spoken, the words in which Jesus speaks of that ineffable relation between the Father and the Son. Then what follows? Does something follow that reveals some later theology of the Church, something that fails to show the unmistakable, characteristic, inimitable quality of Jesus' authentic teaching? Judge for yourselves, my friends. Here is what follows upon that stupendous testimony to the deity of Christ:

"Come unto me, all ye that labour and are heavy laden, and I will give you rest.

"Take my yoke upon you, and learn of me; for I am meek and lowly in heart: and ye shall find rest unto your souls.

"For my yoke is easy, and my burden is light."

Are those the words of some falsifier who put upon the lips of Jesus words that Jesus never spoke? Are those the words of some religious genius who used the name of Jesus as the medium through which he might convey his teaching to the world?

Oh, no, my friends; no religious genius ever spoke

words like these. These are words such as never man spake.

How sweet these words are on the lips of Jesus! How abominable they would be on the lips of any other! "Come unto me, all ye that labour and are heavy laden, and I will give you rest"—who could speak those words without mocking and deceiving those who hear? I will tell you. Only He who said in the same breath: "No man knoweth the Son, but the Father; neither knoweth any man the Father, save the Son." The plain fact is that that gracious invitation of Jesus—an invitation so sweetly repeated again and again in the Gospels by Him who was sent to seek and to save that which was lost—the plain fact is that that invitation is a divine invitation. The one who uttered it was a deceiver or He was God.

Yet, it is objected, there are so many who will not accept the invitation; there are so many learned men who will not believe Jesus when He advances these stupendous claims. Yes, I know. They are very many and they are very learned.

But did not Jesus Himself say so; did not Jesus Himself say that there were many learned persons who would very learnedly reject Him when He offered Himself as their Saviour and Lord? "I thank thee, O Father, Lord of heaven and earth, because thou hast hid these things from the wise and prudent, and hast revealed them unto babes."

Which are you, my friends? Do you belong to the wise and prudent, of whom our Lord spoke? Do you belong to those who rely upon the wisdom of this world and turn aside from Christ? Or are you among the babes? Will you come to Jesus weak and helpless; will you come to Him as a very little child? Are you weary and heavy laden? Will you come to Him that He may give you rest?

XV

THE SUPERNATURAL CHRIST

I HAVE been talking to you about the deity of Christ, and have shown you that Jesus' testimony to His own deity is not found merely in the Gospel according to John. It is found in all four Gospels and it pervades all parts of the Gospels. Even in the so-called ethical parts of the Gospels like the Sermon on the Mount the stupendous claim of Jesus is really presupposed.

We must now, however, notice something else. We must notice that this claim of Jesus is everywhere supported by His power to work miracles. That is the way in which the Gospels represent the miracles. They represent them as attestations to show that Jesus spoke the truth when He came forward with His stupendous claim.

This Biblical estimate of the miracles has often been reversed in the minds of modern men. The miracles, men tell us, even if they really happened, are at best an obstacle to faith rather than an aid to faith. People used to believe, they tell us, because of the miracles; they now believe, if they believe at all, in spite of the miracles.

A curious confusion underlies this way of thinking. In one sense, of course it is true that the miracles are an obstacle to faith. Unquestionably a narrative that has no miracles in it is easier to believe than a narrative that contains miracles. Of course that is so. Who ever denied it? A perfectly trivial narrative is easier to believe than one that contains an account of extraordinary happenings. So if I should tell you that when I walked down the street today I saw a Ford car, my narrative would have at least one advantage over the narratives in the New Testament—it would certainly be far easier to believe. But then it would also have one disadvantage. It would be far easier to believe, but then, you see, it would not be worth believing.

So if the Gospels contained no miracles they would in one sense be easier to believe than they are now. But, do you not see, the thing that would be believed would be entirely different from the thing that is believed now when we take the Gospels as they stand. If the Jesus of the Gospels were a purely natural and not a supernatural person, then we should have no difficulty in believing that such a person lived in the first century of our era. Even skeptics would have no difficulty in believing it. Defenders of the faith would have an easy victory indeed. Everybody would believe. But then there would be one drawback. It would be this— that the thing that everybody would believe would not be worth believing.

A purely natural, as distinguished from a supernatural, Christ would be just a teacher and example. There have been many teachers and examples in the history of mankind. It would place no particular demands upon our faith if we were told that this teacher and example was a little better than any of the others. But then, you see, we are not looking for a teacher and example. We are looking for a Saviour. And a purely human, a merely natural, as distinguished from a supernatural, Christ can never be our Saviour. He would merely be one of us. He would need a Saviour for himself before he could save others; he just as much as we would need a supernatural Saviour.

We have such a Saviour presented to us in the Gospels, a Saviour who is not merely man but God. The really difficult thing to believe is that such a Saviour really entered into this world. It is a very blessed thing, but it is certainly not a trivial thing. It is not one of those trivial things that are so easy to believe because they occur every day. It is certainly not a thing that can be believed without a mighty revolution in all a man's thinking and all a man's life.

If now you ask whether it would be easier to believe *that thing* without the individual miracles narrated in the Gospels than it is to believe it with those individual miracles, we answer emphatically, No. It would be easier to believe the story of a mere religious teacher without the miracles. Certainly. That goes without saying. But not to believe the story of the life upon earth of the incarnate Son of God. The whole appearance of such a divine Person upon earth is itself a stupendous miracle. The individual miracles, with their individual attestation, do make it easier to believe that great central miracle. They are proofs of it. They are exactly what the Bible represents them as being—true testimonies to the truth of that stupendous claim of Jesus to be very God.

If you examine carefully the views of those who reject the individual miracles, you will discover that they do not really hold on to the great central and all-pervading miracle. They may seem to do so. They use the old terminology. They love to speak of "incarnation"; they love to speak of God as having become man. But when you come to look at them closely, you discover that this use of traditional terminology on their part only serves to mask from them themselves and from others a profound difference of thought. They mean by "incarnation" just about the opposite of what the Bible means by it. They do not really mean by it that the eternal Son of God, the second Person of the Trinity, became man this once, and this once only, "and so was, and continueth to be God, and man, in two distinct natures, and one person, for ever." No, they mean something entirely different. They are very far indeed from believing on Christ for salvation as He is offered to us in the gospel.

The truth is that the Bible picture of Jesus possesses a wonderful unity. Without the miracles as the Gospels narrate them the unity would be sadly destroyed. Every one of the miracles, with its historical attestation, adds its quota of evidence to our great central conviction that this Jesus is indeed the Son of God.

It is interesting to observe the way in which the miracles of the life of Christ have been treated in the history of modern unbelief. The cardinal principle of unbelief is that miracles have never happened. What, then, shall be done with the accounts of miracles that are found in the Gospels?

The first impulse of a skeptic might be to say that since the Gospel picture of Jesus contains miracles, and since miracles never happened, therefore the whole picture is untrue. But that of course will not do at all. It is perfectly clear that we have in the Gospels an account of a real person who really lived in Palestine in the first century of our era. The picture is entirely too lifelike ever to have been the product of invention. That is admitted by all except a few extremists. Very well, then. If the picture is the picture of a real person, what shall be done with the miracles that it contains? Those miracles, according to the initial assumption of our skeptical investigator, never happened; yet they are narrated in an account of a real historical person. What shall be done about it?

The obvious answer of unbelievers is that the miracles must be rejected in order to leave the rest. In this way, it is supposed, we shall be able to sift the material in the Gospels in order to arrive at the modicum of truth that they contain. When, it is said, we have removed from the Gospel picture of Jesus these gaudy colors of the supernatural we shall have Jesus as He actually was.

Well, it sounds easy. Surely it must have been accomplished long before now—the removal of the miracles from the picture of Jesus in the Gospels. Many of the most brilliant of modern men have been engaged in it during the past hundred years. Surely their effort must have been successful.

That is certainly what one might expect. But in this case expectations are not borne out by the fact. The plain fact is that this "quest of the historical Jesus," as it has been called—this effort to take the miracles out of the Gospels—has proved to be a colossal failure. It is being increasingly recognized as being a failure even by the skeptical historians themselves. The supernatural is found to be far more deeply rooted in the Gospel account of Jesus than was formerly supposed.

At first, it seemed to be quite easy to get the miracles out of the Gospels. All we shall have to do, said the skeptical historians, is just to take the miracles out and leave all the rest. Even the miracle-incidents themselves, they said, can be accepted as historical; only, we must observe that they were not really miraculous. So Luke

tells us in the first chapter that Zacharias the father of
John the Baptist went into the Temple at the hour of
incense and received an announcement about the birth
of a son. Is that incident historical? Did Zacharias
really go into the Temple that day? Certainly, said the
men of this way of thinking, the incident is historical;
certainly Zacharias went into the Temple. Of course
he was slightly mistaken about what he saw! He
thought he saw an angel when what he really saw was
just the smoke rising from the altar in that dim religious
light. But such mistakes do not cast any general dis-
credit upon the narratives in which they stand.

So also all four of the Gospels say that Jesus one
day fed five thousand men. Is that incident historical?
Did Jesus really feed those five thousand men? Certainly the narrative is historical, said the men of the
way of thinking with which we are now dealing; certainly Jesus fed those five thousand men. What He did
was just to take those five loaves and two fishes and set
a good example by distributing them to the people immediately around Him. That led the other fortunate
people among the crowd to do likewise. His good
example was contagious. People who were fortunate
enough to have any food distributed it to those around
them and so everybody was fed. Thus the incident is
perfectly historical, but it was not really miraculous.
The whole trouble has come from the fact that readers
of the Gospels have insisted on putting a supernatural-

ıstic interpretation upon an incident that was really quite natural.

It is all perfectly easy and simple, is it not? How nicely the task has been accomplished—miracles as neatly extracted as an appendix is extracted in a modern hospital, everything else allowed to remain "as was," the general trustworthiness of the Gospels rescued, Jesus made to keep within the bounds of nature's laws! What was all the bother about? It is all so perfectly simple!

Such was the so-called "rationalizing" method of dealing with the miracle narratives, as practised by Paulus and others one hundred years ago. It had considerable vogue in its day. But its vogue was of short duration. God raised up a besom of destruction for it in the person of a disconcerting young man named David Friedrich Strauss.

Strauss published his "Life of Jesus" in 1835. It was unquestionably one of the most influential books of modern times—a very important book to have been written by a young man of twenty-seven years of age.

I said that Strauss's book was influential. I did not say that its influence was good, and as a matter of fact it was not good but very bad. Strauss did not write in the interests of the truth of the Gospels; he did not write from the point of view of a real Christian believer. On the contrary he wrote from the point of view of an extreme unbelief. His book remains to the present day perhaps the fullest compendium of what can be said against the truthfulness of the Gospel narratives.

Yet such a book had at least the use, in the providence of God, of demolishing the rationalizing method of dealing with the miracle-narratives in the Gospels. In those narratives, Strauss said, the miracles are the main thing; they are the thing for which all the rest exists. How absurd, then, to say that the narratives have grown up out of utterly trivial events upon which a supernaturalistic interpretation was wrongly put! No, said Strauss, we must give up all attempts at finding a modicum of historical truth in these narratives; they are simply myths—that is, they are popular expressions, in narrative form, of certain religious ideas; they are merely the way in which popular fancy expressed the great debt which the early Christian Church owed to Jesus.

At first, Strauss's book caused great consternation. He had not, indeed, denied the historical existence of Jesus, and of course he really held that much that is narrated about Jesus in the Gospels is true. But so radical was his criticism, and so completely did he fail to put together into any continuous positive account of Jesus what was left after his criticism had done its work, that it was quite natural for people to feel that Strauss had almost removed Jesus of Nazareth from the pages of history.

Then, however, an attempt was made to repair the

damage. I am not referring to the defence of the Gospels by believing scholars, but I am referring to the attempt by men of Strauss's own way of thinking—men, that is, who like Strauss denied the occurrence of miracles—to discover and make use of the modicum of truth that might be thought to remain in the Gospels after criticism had been given its rights.

Possibly, it was supposed, that modicum of truth might be discovered by what is called "source-criticism." The Gospels, it was admitted, contain much that is untrue, but if we could discover the earlier sources used by the writers of the Gospels we might get much nearer to the facts. Well, an imposing attempt was made in that direction. The Gospel according to John was rejected as almost altogether unhistorical, and then the two chief sources of Matthew and Luke were held to be (1) Mark and (2) a lost source composed chiefly of sayings of Jesus as distinguished from accounts of His deeds. That was the famous "two-document theory" as to the sources of the Gospels.

On the basis of that theory a supposedly historical account of a purely human Jesus was constructed. People became quite enthusiastic about it. The troublesome miracles, it was supposed, were all removed; the theological Christ of the creeds was done away. But, it was said, something better had been rediscovered—a really and purely human Jesus, a Jesus who was one of us, a Jesus who started where we started and won through to sonship with God, a Jesus who kept His own person out of His gospel and simply taught—by word and by life —the great liberating truths of the fatherhood of God and the brotherhood of man.

Such was the so-called "Liberal Jesus." It was an imposing reconstruction indeed. It was thought to offer great promise to the human race. The shackles of dogma, it was supposed, had been removed. A new Reformation would soon take place.

But alas for human hopes! Nothing has been seen of the new Reformation, and the imposing reconstruction of the Liberal Jesus has fallen to the ground. I think the first thirty-five years of the twentieth century might almost be called, in the sphere of New Testament criticism, the period of the decline and fall of "the Liberal Jesus." That is a great outstanding fact. I think that it is a fact that is going to loom up very large to future historians when the history of the period in which we are living comes finally to be written.

The great trouble is that the miraculous in the Gospels is found to be much more pervasive than it was at first thought to be. It runs through the Gospels as we now have them. That is clear. But it also is found to run through the sources supposed rightly or wrongly to underlie the Gospels. All right, then; suppose we go even back of those earliest written sources and examine supposed detached bits of oral tradition out of which they are sometimes supposed to have been composed. Alas, we obtain no relief. Those supposed detached bits are found themselves to contain the objectionable miraculous element. There seems to be no escape from the supernatural Christ. At the very beginning of the Church—not at some later time but at the very beginning—Jesus was regarded not just as a religious teacher or just as a prophet but as a supernatural Deliverer.

That is the result at which ultra-modern criticism has arrived. It is a far cry from the cheerful, rationalizing days of Paulus one hundred years ago. It is a far cry from the time when men thought they could explain away this miracle-narrative and that, and have a perfectly good account left of a great religious teacher.

The outstanding result of a hundred years of effort to separate the natural from the supernatural in the early Christian view of Jesus is that the thing cannot be done. The two are inseparable. The very earliest early Christian account of Jesus is found to be supernaturalistic to the core.

Very well, what shall we do about it? The earliest view of Jesus that we know anything about represents Him as a supernatural person. It is found to exhibit a remarkable unanimity at this point. What shall we do with it? There are only two things to do with it. We can take it or we can leave it.

Modern skeptical historians are saying we must leave it. All our information about Jesus is supernaturalistic, they are saying; therefore all our information about Jesus is uncertain. We can never disentangle the real Jesus from the beliefs of His earliest followers. The only Christ we really know is the supernatural Christ of Jesus' earliest followers. We can never rediscover the portrait of the real Jesus.

Are you afraid of skepticism like that? I am not afraid of it a bit. It is easily refuted by a mere reading of the Gospels. I beg you just to read the Gospels for yourselves, my friends, and then ask yourselves whether the Person there presented to you is not a living, breathing person. The extreme skepticism of the day will always be refuted by common sense.

That being so, the extreme skepticism of our day is very instructive. I get great comfort from it. Do you not see, my friends? That extreme skepticism of Bultmann and others is the inevitable result of trying to reject the miracles in the Gospels. That extreme skepticism is absurd. What is the conclusion? The conclusion is that the process which inevitably led to that extreme skepticism was wrong from the beginning. We never ought to have tried to reject the miracles in the Gospels at all.

I wonder when men are going to draw this conclusion. It does seem to lie so very near at hand. When will they cease to be blind to it? The Gospels present to us just one Christ—the supernatural Christ. They do so with overwhelmingly self-evidencing force. When shall we just accept their witness? When shall we just say that God did walk upon this earth? When shall we just come to that divine Christ and ask Him to be the Saviour of our souls?

XVI

DID CHRIST RISE FROM THE DEAD? [1]

In the last of these talks, I was speaking to you about the miracles of Christ. But a treatment of the miracles would be incomplete unless we singled out for special examination the central or crowning miracle, which is the miracle of the resurrection.

In treating the resurrection, I suggest that we may begin with things about which everybody is agreed, in order that we may go on from them to speak of things with regard to which Christian people differ from those who are not Christians.

Nineteen hundred years ago there lived in an obscure corner of the Roman Empire one who would have seemed to a superficial observer to be a remarkable man. He engaged in a career of religious teaching accompanied by a ministry of healing. At first He had the favor of the crowd, but since He would not be the kind of leader the people demanded He soon fell victim to the jealousy of the rulers of His people and to the

---

[1] The subject of this address was similarly, but somewhat more fully, treated in a lecture on "The Resurrection," which was published in *Winona Echoes* for 1924 and in *The Bible To-day* for April and May, 1925.

cowardice of the Roman governor. He died the death of criminals of that day, on the cross.

At His death, His followers were discouraged. They had evidently been far inferior to Him in discernment and in courage, and now what little courage they may have had was gone. His death meant the destruction of all their hopes. Never, one might have said, was a movement more completely dead than the movement which had been begun by Jesus of Nazareth.

Then, however, the surprising thing happened. It is a fact of history, which no real historian denies, that those same weak discouraged men, the followers of Jesus, began, within a very short time after the shameful death of their leader, in Jerusalem, the scene of their cowardly flight, the most remarkable religious movement that the world has ever known, the movement commonly called the Christian Church.

At first, that movement was obscure. But it spread like wildfire. In a few decades at the most it was firmly planted in the chief cities of the civilized world and in Rome itself. After a lapse of less than three centuries it conquered the Roman Empire. Incalculable has been its influence upon the whole history of the world.

What caused that remarkable change in those followers of Jesus? What caused those weak and cowardly men suddenly to become the spiritual conquerors of the world?

At that point the difference of opinion arises. Yet

even with regard to that point there is a certain measure of agreement. It is now admitted by historians both Christian and non-Christian that those followers of Jesus became the founders of what is commonly known as the Christian Church because they became honestly convinced that Jesus was risen from the dead.

But what in turn produced that conviction? What produced the belief of the first disciples in the resurrection of Christ? There is where the difference of opinion comes in.

The New Testament, of course, has a perfectly clear answer to the question. The belief of the disciples in the resurrection, according to the New Testament, was due simply to the fact of the resurrection. Those disciples came to believe that Jesus had risen from the dead for the simple reason that Jesus *had* risen from the dead. He had risen from the dead; and they had not only seen His tomb empty but had seen Him Himself alive after His death on the cross.

If that explanation of the belief of the first disciples in the resurrection be rejected, what shall be put into its place? The answer to that question which is given today by all or practically all unbelievers is that those first disciples of Jesus became convinced that Jesus had risen from the dead because they experienced certain hallucinations, certain pathological experiences in which they thought they saw Jesus before their eyes when in reality there was nothing there. In an hallucination, the optic nerve is really affected; but it is affected not by light rays coming from an external object, but by some pathological condition of the bodily organism of the subject himself. This is the so-called "vision theory" regarding the origin of the Christian Church. It has held the field among unbelievers inside of the Church and outside of the Church since the days of Strauss about one hundred years ago.

I think we ought to understand just exactly what that vision theory means. It means that the Christian Church is founded upon a pathological experience of certain persons in the first century of our era. It means that if there had been a good neurologist for Peter and the others to consult there never would have been a Christian Church

I am perfectly well aware of the fact that advocates of the vision hypothesis refuse to look at the matter just exactly in that way. The really important thing, they say, was not the pathological experience which those men had, but it was the impression left upon them by Jesus' character. They never would have experienced those hallucinations, they say, unless their minds and hearts had been filled with the thought of the radiant personality of Jesus. It was because they were so much impressed with Him that they came to have those hallucinations. Thus the hallucinations, say the advocates of the vision hypothesis, were merely the temporary form which was necessary in that day and among men of that kind of education in order that the influence of Jesus could continue to make itself felt. *We,* they say, can get rid of that form. We no longer need to believe that Jesus rose from the dead and appeared to the eyes of His disciples. But we can still let the influence of Jesus be felt in our lives. In the changed lives of men who have been influenced by Him Jesus has His truest resurrection.

So the thing is represented by the advocates of what is misleadingly called a "spiritual resurrection." This representation altogether ignores the real character of the first disciples' faith. What those men had from the appearances of the risen Christ was not merely the conviction that Jesus was still alive. No, what they had was the conviction that He had risen. It was not merely the *state* of Jesus resultant upon the resurrection which was valuable for them, but the act of the resurrection. At the heart of their faith was the conviction that Jesus had *done* something for them by His death and resurrection. The Christian religion in other words is rooted in an event.

If that supposed event really took place, as the Bible says it did, then the Christian religion is true. If it did not take place, as the dominant vision theory holds, then the Christian religion is false, and a Church that professes it is merely an empty shell.

But is the message upon which the Christian Church is founded really true? Did Christ rise from the dead?

I want to say just a few words to you about that subject now

Two things are to be noted about the account of the appearances which the New Testament contains.

The first thing concerns the manner of the appearances. The appearances, according to the New Testament, were of a plain bodily kind. Jesus did not, it is true, simply resume the conditions of His life before the crucifixion. There was something mysterious about His coming and going. Yet He is plainly represented as being with His disciples in body They could touch Him. He partook of food in their presence He held extended conversations with them.

The second feature of the appearances, as they are described in the New Testament, concerns the place of the appearances. The appearances, according to the New Testament, were both at Jerusalem and in Galilee; and the first appearances were at Jerusalem.

Both these features of the New Testament account of the appearances are rejected by advocates of the vision hypothesis. The former feature is always rejected by them, the latter usually

The advocates of the vision hypothesis hold, with regard to the manner of the appearances, that, contrary to the New Testament, the appearances were only of a momentary kind. The disciples who experienced the appearances did not experience any extended intercourse with Jesus. They not only did not *really* have any extended intercourse with Him, but they did not even *think* they had any extended intercourse with Him. All they even thought they had was a momentary sight of Him in glory or perhaps the sound of a word or two of His ringing in their ears. The New Testament is quite wrong in saying they even thought they saw or heard any more than that.

The second point at which the advocates of the vision hypothesis, or most of them, reject the New Testament account of the appearances concerns the place of the appearances. Most of the advocates of the vision hypothesis hold that the first of the "appearances"—which they of course regard as hallucinations—took place a considerable time, perhaps weeks, after the crucifixion, in Galilee; the New Testament says that the first of the appearances took place at Jerusalem on the third day after the death of Jesus.

At first sight it might look as though this were a mere difference in detail. But that is not so. As a matter of fact it is a difference of a very important kind.

If the first appearances, the first of these supposed hallucinations in which the disciples thought they saw Jesus alive after His death, took place at Jerusalem and on the third day after the death, then the question arises why the tomb of Jesus was not investigated to see whether the story of the resurrection was really true— why it was not investigated by foes as well as by friends.

If the resurrection was not a fact, then the investigation of the tomb of Jesus would refute the story, and the beginning of the Christian Church would have been prevented.

If, on the other hand, the first appearances took place in Galilee weeks after the death of Jesus, then, it might be said, when the disciples finally did return to Jerusalem it would be too late for the tomb to be investigated Thus the so-called Galilean hypothesis as to the place of the first appearances might be thought to remove the difficulty which a consideration of the tomb of Jesus has always placed in the way of a denial of the fact of the resurrection

What shall be said about that? Two things are to be said about it

In the first place, even the Galilean hypothesis does not really remove the difficulty, since it does seem strange even on the Galilean hypothesis that the tomb of Jesus was not investigated, and, in the second place the Galilean hypothesis is not true

Where shall we turn to test the hypothesis of unbelievers not only on this point regarding the place of the appearances but also on the point regarding the manner of the appearances?

Well, we can of course turn to the Gospels We can show that the low view which unbelievers hold regarding the Gospels is not justified and that these docu-

ments are really trustworthy accounts of what the first
disciples of Jesus said with regard to the founding of
the Church.

But obviously it would be a good thing also if we
could find some source of information which is admitted to be good not only by believers but also by unbelievers. Can we find such a source of information?
Can we find a source of information with regard to
which there is some common meeting ground between
ourselves and our opponents in this debate?

The answer is, Yes. We can find such a source of
information in the First Epistle to the Corinthians. It is
generally admitted by foes of our view as well as by
friends that that Epistle was really written by the
Apostle Paul and that it was written at about A.D. 55,
approximately twenty-five years after the death of Jesus.
It is also generally admitted that when Paul says in
this Epistle that he had "received" the information that
he gives in the fifteenth chapter regarding the resurrection and appearances of Jesus he means that he had received it from the early Jerusalem Church—particularly,
perhaps, from Peter, with whom he tells us in another
of his Epistles that he spent fifteen days only three years
after his conversion. What we have here, then, in the
fifteenth chapter of this Epistle, in verse eight and the
following verses, is a precious bit of what modern historians call "primitive tradition." It is usually admitted by friends and foes of our view that we have

here a summary of what the very earliest Jerusalem Church said about the events that lay at the beginning of its life.

Well, then, is this account by the primitive Jerusalem Church of the resurrection and related events favorable to the contention of unbelievers—the contention that at the beginning the appearances were regarded as independent of what had become of the body of Jesus? Volumes have been written about this question. But the answer, if we may put it plainly and briefly, is most emphatically, No. This passage is not favorable to the contention of unbelievers at all.

What does Paul say exactly when he summarizes that precious tradition of the earliest Jerusalem Church? Here is what he says:

"For I delivered unto first of all that which I also received, how that Christ died for our sins according to the Scriptures; and that he was buried, and that he rose again the third day according to the Scriptures."

I want you to notice the mention of the burial of Christ in this passage. What does it mean? I will tell you, and then I just want you to read the passage for yourselves to see whether you do not agree with me. When Paul mentions the burial, he means that the resurrection of Christ about which he is speaking is a bodily resurrection. The thing that was laid in the tomb in the burial was the body; and the thing that was laid in the tomb was the thing that came out of the tomb in the resurrection. "He died, He was buried, He rose." We follow here, as we read, what happened to the body of Jesus. If a man will just read the words without prejudice he will see that they are at this point as plain as day.

It is quite clear that Paul does not mean, and the Jerusalem Church as quoted by him did not mean, that the body of Jesus remained in the tomb. The bodily resurrection is the only resurrection that the New Testament knows.

In fact, when we come to think about it, a resurrection that is not a bodily resurrection is a contradiction in terms. Did those first disciples, when they began the work of the Christian Church, merely believe in the continued personal existence of Jesus? Was that what gave them their strange new confidence and power? Such a view is really quite absurd. They had *that* conviction even in the sad hours immediately after the crucifixion. They were not Sadducees. They believed in the personal survival of all men after death; and so they believed, even just after the crucifixion, in the personal survival of Jesus. But that conviction left them in despair. What changed their despair into joy was the substitution, in their minds, for a belief in the continued personal existence of Jesus, of a belief in His resurrection. It is quite absurd, then, to say that the two things, in their view, were the same. Our sources of information about the beginnings of the Christian Church know nothing whatever of a resurrection that is not a bodily resurrection.

The second thing that I want you to notice in the report by Paul of the tradition of the Jerusalem Church is the mention of the third day. "And that He rose again the third day according to the Scriptures," he says. There are few words in the whole Bible that are more uncomfortable to modern unbelief than those words "the third day" in the primitive Jerusalem tradition recorded here by Paul.

Those words demolish the whole edifice of the Galilean hypothesis as to the place of the appearances. They show, by the testimony of the very first disciples, that the first appearance did *not* take place in Galilee weeks after the crucifixion but on the third day and at Jerusalem. I know that attempts are made to evade the plain implications of these words. The first appearances, it is said, took place only weeks afterwards, but when they did take place the disciples who experienced them hit upon the notion that Jesus had risen long before and merely had not chosen to appear to them until then. But why in the world did they hit upon just the third day as the day of the resurrection if nothing in particular happened to them on that day? Various answers have been given to that question, but they are vain. No, the mention of the third day in the primitive Jerusalem tradition interposes a mighty barrier against the whole attempt to explain the appearances of the risen Christ as hallucinations experienced at a time when it would be too late to investigate the tomb of Jesus to see whether the resurrection had really happened or not.

The truth is that the origin of the Church in Jerusalem is explicable if Jesus really rose from the dead, and it is not explicable if He did not so rise. The very existence of the Christian Church is a mighty testimony to the resurrection of our Lord.

But, it will be objected, that is all very well, but the trouble is that the thing we are asked to believe is really unbelievable. We are asked to believe that a dead man rose from the dead, and we have never seen a man who did that.

What is our answer to this objection? It is very simple. You say, my friend, that you have never seen a man who rose from the dead after he had been laid really dead in the tomb? Quite right. Neither have I. You and I have never seen a man who rose from the dead. That is true. But what of it? You and I have never seen a man who rose from the dead; but then you and I have never seen a man like Jesus.

Do you not see, my friends? What we are trying to establish is not the resurrection of any ordinary man, not the resurrection of a man who is to us a mere x or y not the resurrection of a man about whom we know nothing, but the resurrection of Jesus. There is a tremendous presumption against the resurrection of any ordinary man, but when you come really to know Jesus as He is pictured to us in the Gospels you will say that whereas it is unlikely that any ordinary man should rise from the dead, in His case the presumption is exactly reversed. It is unlikely that any ordinary man should rise; but it is unlikely that *this* man should not rise; it may be said of this man that it was impossible that He should be holden of death.

The point is that this thing hangs together. We have in the Gospels an account of a Person who was entirely unique. He was totally different from other men in His moral purity and strength. Yet He made the most stupendous claims—claims that place Him beyond the bounds of sanity unless the claims were true. The claims are true if the resurrection really happened; they are a hopeless puzzle if the resurrection did not happen.

Do you see what I am driving at, my friends? The evidence of the truth of Christianity must be taken as a whole. The direct evidence for the resurrection must be taken together with the total picture of Jesus in the Gospels, and then that must be taken in connection with the evidence for the existence of God and the tremendous need of man which is caused by sin. If you take the Bible as a whole you have a grand consistent account of God, of the world and of human life. If you reject the Bible, and particularly if you reject the fact of the resurrection, you have a jumble of meaningless and detached bits of information that dance before your imagination in a wild and riotous rout.

Oh, that God would open men's eyes that they might see, that they might detect the grand sweep and power of His testimony to Himself in His Word! Oh, that He would take away the terrible blindness of men's minds! Has He taken away the blindness of *your* minds, my friends? Do you know the risen Christ today as your Saviour and your Lord? If you do not yet know Him, will you not bow before Him at this hour and say, "My Lord and my God!"

XVII

THE TESTIMONY OF PAUL TO CHRIST [1]

In our presentation of the testimony of the New Testament to the deity of Christ, we have dealt so far only with the Gospels But now it becomes necessary to consider also the other New Testament books and particularly the Epistles of Paul

The reason why the Epistles of Paul are particularly important in this connection is that with regard to them we find a common meeting ground with those who deny the deity of Christ and are opposed to the Christian religion. Practically all serious literary critics today admit that the principal ones of the Pauline Epistles were really written by the man whose name they bear

In the case of the four Gospels it is not so easy to find a common meeting ground with our opponents We did not indeed altogether give up the hope of finding it We tried to point out that there is a certain amount of agreement even with regard to the Gospels between those who are friends and those who are foes of Christianity. It is universally admitted, for example,

[1] For a fuller treatment of this subject by the same writer, see *The Origin of Paul's Religion,* 1921

by serious historians, that the picture of Jesus in the Gospels is a picture of a real, historical person. We tried to point out certain important consequences that follow from that admission. But, after all, the common meeting ground which we can find with our opponents is, so far as the Gospels are concerned, not very extensive.

In particular, there is disagreement with regard to questions of what is known as "literary criticism." There is disagreement, namely, with regard to the authorship and date and historical value of each of the Gospels. If, therefore, we begin by assuming that any one of these Gospels was written by the man whose name has been attached to it in the opinion of the Church, we shall be accused at once of begging the question. The traditional view of the authorship of all four of these books is disputed by our opponents in this great debate.

Now, mind you, I do not think that it is rightly disputed. I am perfectly willing to defend the traditional view of the authorship of the Gospels. I think it is immensely important to defend it. I think it can successfully be defended. But the point is that it *needs* to be defended. Rightly or wrongly the traditional view of the authorship of the Gospels is disputed by modern skeptics.

About the Epistles of Paul, on the other hand, there is no such dispute. Even the most skeptical critics—except a few extremists who are altogether without influence upon the current of modern thought—admit that the principal ones of the Pauline Epistles were really written by the Apostle Paul and written in the first generation of the Christian Church.

That is a very important admission indeed. I think it is very important that we should use it in our effort to lead the men who make it to accept the claims of Christ. You see, we do not regard the people who differ from us regarding these great concerns of the soul as our enemies. On the contrary, we long to help them. Having known something of the misery of doubt ourselves, we long to help others out of that misery. Hence we do like, if we can, to find a common meeting ground with our opponents in the debate, in order that we may lead them on from the things about which they agree with us to an acceptance of the things about which they disagree.

It is to be welcomed, therefore, that friends and foes of Christianity are agreed in holding that the principal ones of the Pauline Epistles were really written by the Apostle Paul.

The man, Paul, who wrote those Epistles was a contemporary of Jesus. That can be shown from the accepted Epistles themselves, because Paul in the Epistle to the Galatians says that he himself had met a brother of Jesus and it is very clear that this meeting took place only a short time after Jesus' death. Paul had abundant opportunities to learn the facts about Jesus. He spent fifteen days, as he tells us in Galatians, with Peter, who was in the innermost circle of Jesus' friends, and at the same time he also saw James, who was Jesus' brother. Contact with the same men was also established at the later time that is referred to in the second chapter of Galatians, and at that later time John, who, like Peter, belonged to Jesus' innermost circle of friends, was also present. Barnabas and Silas, who, according to the Book of Acts came from the early Jerusalem Church, were associated with Paul through long periods of time on the missionary journeys; and while it may be objected that our knowledge of their original connection with the Jerusalem Church comes only from the Book of Acts and not from the universally accepted Epistles of Paul, still the historical basis of such concrete personal details in the Book of Acts will be admitted probably by most critics. At any rate it is perfectly clear, in view of all the conditions of Paul's life, that Paul had abundant contacts with those who had known Jesus when He was on earth.

The testimony of Paul to Jesus becomes, therefore, a matter of the highest importance to every careful historian who is interested in the beginnings of the Christian Church. It becomes very important for us to ask what sort of person Paul held Jesus to be.

The answer to that question is very surprising to anyone who approaches the subject with ordinary analogies in his mind, because it becomes perfectly clear at once that Paul regarded Jesus in a very extraordinary way. He regarded Him as a supernatural person and he regarded himself as standing to Jesus in the relation in which a man stands to God.

He does, it is true, speak of Jesus as a man. But when he speaks of Him as a man we may well hold that he regarded it as something extraordinary, something un-expected, that He should be a man. The really out-standing thing in the way in which Paul speaks of Jesus is that he separates Jesus very clearly from ordinary humanity and places Him on the side of God.

So at the beginning of the Epistle to the Galatians, for example, he says that he, Paul, is an apostle not from men nor through a man but through Jesus Christ and God the Father who raised Him from the dead. *"Not* through a man *but* through Jesus Christ!"* Man is one thing, Christ another; and Christ, over against man, is placed with God the Father. Could there be any clearer testimony to the deity of Christ?

In one place at least Paul applies to Jesus the Greek word which is translated by the English word "God." I am referring to Rom. 9:5, where Christ is spoken of as the one "who is over all, God blessed for ever." At-tempts have been made to avoid holding that the word "God" in this passage refers to Christ, but it is more than doubtful whether any of those attempts can be regarded as successful. According to the plain construction of the words, the construction which in any other case would be regarded by every reader as a matter of course, Paul here calls Jesus "God."

It is true that ordinarily he does not use that word in speaking of Christ. He does not ordinarily apply to Christ the word which is translated "God" in our English Bibles. But what of it? He does apply to Christ constantly another word which can clearly be shown to be a word designating deity—namely, the word "Lord." That word had, indeed, its uses in ordinary life; it designated a master of slaves and the like. But it had also a widespread religious use, and—what is vastly more important—it is the word used in the Greek translation of the Old Testament (which was the form of the Bible that Paul ordinarily employed) to translate the word "Jehovah," the holiest name of the covenant God of Israel; and Paul does not hesitate to apply to Jesus Old Testament passages that speak of Jehovah.

In view of this lofty significance of the word "Lord" Dr. B. B. Warfield is surely justified when he suggests that the title "the Lord" may almost be designated as Paul's "Trinitarian name" of Jesus Christ.[2] Paul teaches the doctrine of the Trinity—only, as Dr. Warfield points out, he uses a somewhat different terminology from that to which we have become accustomed. Instead of speaking of "God the Father, God the Son and

[2] Warfield, *The Lord of Glory*, 1907, p. 231.

God the Holy Ghost," He speaks of "God," "the Lord" and "the Spirit"; but he teaches exactly the same doctrine as that which is taught when men use that other terminology. And His doctrine of the Trinity includes, of course, the doctrine of the deity of Christ.

The doctrine of the deity of Christ is all-pervasive in the Epistles of Paul. It is by no means an isolated thing. You do not have to search for it to find it. On the contrary, you cannot get away from it. Open the Epistles where you will and you will find the deity of Christ.

Take, for example, the way in which Paul speaks of Christ in the openings of almost all of his Epistles. "Grace to you and peace," he says, "from God our Father and the Lord Jesus Christ." [8] Those words often make little impression on our minds. We trip along very lightly over them. But why is it that they make no impression on our minds; why is it that we trip along so lightly over them? Simply for the reason that we have become accustomed to them. They do not stand out in any way in the Epistles of Paul because they are so completely in accord with all that Paul says elsewhere about Christ. But in themselves they are really most extraordinary words. Imagine it being said about any other man who ever lived—the greatest of reformers or the holiest of saints—"Grace to you and

[8] See the article by B. B. Warfield, "God Our Father and the Lord Jesus Christ," in *Princeton Theological Review*, xv, 1917, pp. 1-20, reprinted in *Biblical Doctrines*, 1929, pp. 215-231.

peace from God our Father and Martin Luther, or the Apostle Paul himself or John the Beloved Disciple"—and I think you will see at once how blasphemous such a form of words would be. Why is it not blasphemous, then, when Paul says "Grace be with you and peace from God our Father and the Lord Jesus Christ"? For one reason and one reason only, my friends. Because Jesus Christ is God. Being God, and for that reason only, He can be linked in this stupendous fashion with God the Father and can be separated from the whole universe of created things.

The reason why we think nothing of those stupendous words as we come to them at the beginnings of the Epistles is that they are in exact accord with *everything* that Paul says about Jesus. The reason why they do not stand out like mountain peaks in the Epistles is not that they are not high but that everything else that Paul says about Christ is equally high.

Then I want you to understand something else about the way in which Paul teaches the deity of Christ. It is this—that Paul's teaching about the deity of Christ is not found merely in this passage or that. It is not found merely in any number of passages where Paul ascribes divine honor and glory to Christ—no matter how numerous you may find those passages to be. No, Paul teaches the deity of Christ by the inmost heart and core of his own religious life.

What was the religion of Paul really like? We ought

to be able to get the answer to that question, because Paul had a remarkable gift of self-revelation. Someone, I believe, has said that he is the best known man of antiquity. He has bared his heart to us in his Epistles. He appears there not as a cold academic teacher but as a man of flesh and blood, and he has let us know what were the inmost springs of his life.

Evidently those springs of his life were in his religion. There never was a more intensely religious man.

What then was that religion of Paul—that religion of Paul that is so wonderfully presented to us in those revealing documents, the Epistles?

Did that religion of Paul consist in having faith in God like the faith which Jesus had in God? Was Jesus for Paul just an example for faith—just a pioneer in the religious life, just one who attained sonship with God and inspired others to attain it?

Well, some people have tried to look at the thing in that way. But they have done so only by closing their eyes to what actually stands in the documents from which our information is to be derived. If you simply close your eyes and construct out of your own inner consciousness what you think Paul *ought* to have said, then of course you can make Paul out to be an adherent of what men call "the religion of Jesus"; you can make him out to be a man whose religion consisted primarily in an imitation of the religious experience through which Jesus Himself had passed; you can make him out to be a man whose religion consisted in an effort to have the same kind of faith in God as that faith which Jesus had in God.

But the moment you allow yourself to be hampered in the flight of your imagination by some knowledge of the facts, the moment you seek to view Paul not as you think he ought to have been but as he was, you will observe that his religion did not consist merely in the effort to have the same kind of faith in God as the faith which Jesus had, but that it consisted in having faith in Jesus. Jesus, according to Paul, was no mere example for faith, but was the object of faith. He was the object, for Paul, of a faith that was truly religious. What does that mean? It means plainly one thing. It means that Paul stood toward Jesus not just in the relation in which a disciple stands toward his teacher, but in the relation in which a man stands toward his God. The deity of Christ is the foundation of Paul's life.

In the light of this fact, we are not surprised to read what Paul says about Christ in detail. Jesus Christ, according to Paul, existed from all eternity. He was the One through whom the universe was made. He came into this world as a man not as other men come but by a voluntary act—an act of wonderful condescension and love. His death was not just a noble martyrdom but an act of cosmic significance. It meant the redemption, from the wrath and curse of God, of a great multitude of men of all nations. After His death, He rose from the dead and is now exalted far above all principalities and powers. He belongs with God the Father in a category entirely distinct from that of all created things.

Have you ever stopped just to think how extraordinary that Pauline doctrine of the deity of Christ would seem to you to be if you came to it for the first time? Here was Jesus, a man who had lived only a few years before and had died a shameful death. Here was Paul, a contemporary of Jesus, an associate of Jesus' intimate friends, yet attributing to Jesus the highest divine attributes, and standing to Him always in the relation in which a man stands to God.

Have you ever heard of anything like that anywhere else in the history of the human race? Perhaps you might be tempted to say, Yes. Perhaps you might be tempted to say that this was not the first time or the only time in the history of the world when one man has attributed deity to another. There was the deification of the Roman emperors, for example, and the deification of oriental monarchs.

But do you not see the stupendous difference, my friends? Those who deified the Roman emperors were polytheists; they believed in many gods. There was nothing extraordinary, therefore, in their believing that one more god was to be added to the great host of gods with which earth and heaven were already peopled. Paul, on the other hand, was a monotheist. He believed that there was one God and one God only, the Maker of heaven and earth. He was a Jew, and the Jews were nothing if not monotheists. Both before and after his conversion the belief in one God was the very breath of his life. With all his soul he hated the very thought that any other could be called God save that One.

Yet it was such a monotheist sprung of a race of monotheists who paid to one of his contemporaries, Jesus, honors that belong only to God, who reposed in Him a truly religious faith, who applied to Him Old Testament passages that spoke of Jehovah the covenant God of Israel, the one living and true God, the God who in the beginning created the heavens and the earth.

No, there is nothing like that in the whole history of mankind, nothing like that ascription of deity to the man Christ Jesus by the Apostle Paul. It is no wonder that H. J. Holtzmann, ablest representative, perhaps, of the unbelief of the nineteenth and beginning of the twentieth century, admitted that for the deification of the man Jesus as it appears in the Epistles of Paul he was able to cite no parallel in the religious history of the race.[4]

I tell you, my friends, it is only ignorance that can trip along lightly over this amazing phenomenon. Real scholars are at least immensely intrigued by it.

But so far I have not mentioned what is the most surprising thing of all about it. The truly amazing thing

[4] H. J. Holtzmann, in *Protestantische Monatshefte*, iv, 1900, pp. 465 f., and in *Christliche Welt*, xxiv, 1910, column 153.

is not merely that Paul believed in the deity of Christ, but that he does not argue about it; the truly amazing thing is that he seems to treat it as a matter of course. About other things there was bitter debate. There was debate, for example, about the place of the Law in the attainment of salvation. About that opponents of Paul appealed to Peter and the original apostles of Jesus against Paul. Even about that, indeed, their appeal was a false appeal. The original apostles were really with Paul and against those Judaizers. But about the deity of Christ the Judaizers evidently did not make any appeal at all. Paul just assumes that everyone in the Church, including his opponents, will agree with his stupendous view of Jesus Christ. Still more clearly does he assume that the original friends of Jesus will agree with it. That is the truly extraordinary thing. The intimate friends of Jesus—think of it—those who had walked and talked with Him when He was on earth, those who had seen Him subject to all the petty limitations of human life—these intimate friends of Jesus stood, so far as we can see from the Epistles of Paul, in the most complete agreement in their view of Jesus with one who regarded Jesus as very God.

Who was this Jesus who was exalted to the throne of God not by later generations but by His own intimate friends? The Gospels give the only believable answer to that question. Their picture of Jesus is independent of Paul; it is certainly not just spun out of what the Pauline Epistles say about Christ. Yet it presents just the Christ whom the Epistles presuppose.

Deny the truthfulness of the Gospel picture of Jesus, and you can never explain the origin of the religion of Paul. Take the picture as it stands, and all is clear. The two great testimonies to Christ—the Gospels and Paul —lead to the same end. And at that end of the testimony we find the Saviour of our souls.

XVIII

THE HOLY SPIRIT

IN bringing this little series of addresses now to a close, I want to say what a great pleasure it has been to me to become acquainted with you. Our conversations might, indeed, seem at first sight to have been just a little bit one-sided; in them I have done most of the talking. I hope you will not be unkind enough to say that that is the reason why I have enjoyed the conversations so much. I will confess that I do love to talk about these themes with which we have been dealing; but then, you see, I have also enjoyed the companionship I have had with you. These are rather trying days to a man who sorrows when a visible Church that professes to believe the Word of God turns from it so often into the pathways of unbelief and sin; and in such days it is doubly comforting to converse with those who truly love the Gospel of Christ and believe that it alone is the message that is forever new. I do rejoice with all my heart in the Christian fellowship which we have had together, and I trust that God may richly bless you, both in joy and in sorrow, and may by His Holy Spirit cause you always to be grounded upon the rock of His holy Word.

231

One thing is clear, my friends—the Word of God will never fail. Many, indeed, have turned from it in our day. Religious presecution is going on apace in Russia and in Germany and in Mexico; in those countries unbelief is blatant and unashamed and is endeavoring to stamp out the Christian religion by force. In our country the same tendency, though in less extreme form, is already mightily at work; and the visible Church is often unfaithful to its great trust and in some cases is engaged in driving out real Christian testimony from its communion.

But this is not the first time of discouragement in the history of the Christian Church, and sometimes the darkest hour has just preceded the dawn. So it may be in our day. Let us never forget that the Spirit of God, who inspired the writers of the Bible, is all-powerful, and that He can make even dead churches to live.

Then I want to say a word of farewell also to any of you who have disagreed with what I have been trying to say. I appreciate your being broad-minded enough to listen to that with which you do not agree; and I do trust that, if I have not been able to convince you of the truth of what I have been saying, God may send you a messenger of His own choosing who is better fitted than I to proclaim to you that truth which I have so imperfectly proclaimed.

It must be admitted, as we come to the last talk of this little series, that the title of the series is something of a fraud. It is not an intentional fraud, to be sure; but still an unkind person might say that it is a fraud. I have certainly not succeeded in treating "The Christian Faith in the Modern World" in any comprehensive way. Indeed I have made only a bare beginning of treating it. I have spoken of the Bible, from which the Christian Faith is derived, and I have spoken of the Biblical doctrine of God. But I have not treated all the divisions even of that latter topic. I have spoken a little of the Trinity, but can only—in the present talk—touch slightly upon the last part of that great subject; and I have not been able to speak, for example, of the decrees of God at all.

As for the other parts of the system of doctrine that the Bible contains, I have not been able even to make a beginning of treating them. I have not spoken of the Biblical doctrine of man and of sin; I have not spoken of the Biblical doctrine of salvation. I hope to be able to deal with those themes at some future time. Meanwhile I can just bid you turn to God's Word and read it for yourselves. Doing that, after all, is far more worth while than listening to expositions even though they were far better than mine. May the Holy Spirit increasingly unfold to you the boundless treasures of truth that the Bible contains!

As I utter that prayer, I am brought to the theme that it would be next in order for me to deal with in our little series of talks. That theme would be the teach-

ing of the Bible concerning the Holy Spirit. I have
talked to you just a little about the Father, and I have
tried to present to you just a little of what the Bible says
about the Son, but so far I have not spoken to you spe-
cifically about the Third Person of the Trinity, the Holy
Spirit. Please do not understand by that neglect that I
do not think the subject is important.

If only I had time I might naturally treat that subject
much more fully than it can be treated now

Even if I did have more time, I should not, indeed,
give as much time to that subject as I should give, for
example, to the subject of the deity of Christ. Devout
persons sometimes seem to think that there is something
derogatory to the third person of the Trinity, the Holy
Spirit, in the fact that theologians and preachers do not
devote so much time or space to the doctrine of the
Holy Spirit as they do to the doctrine of the deity of
Christ. These persons are apt, I think, to be particularly severe on the so-called "Apostles' Creed," for
example, because, after it has set forth a number of
facts about Christ, the only thing that it says about the
third person of the Trinity is just the bare clause, "I
believe in the Holy Ghost." Surely that extreme brevity,
they will be inclined to say, is derogatory to the third
person of the Trinity, who is equal in power and glory
to the Father and the Son.

Well, I do not know whether we ought to be so very
hard on the Apostles' Creed at this point. No doubt it

is defective—at this point as at a good many other points. No doubt it ought to say something more about the Holy Spirit than just "I believe in the Holy Ghost." But after all the work of the Holy Spirit is especially to witness to the Son and to the Father. So, although the Bible has a great deal to say about the work of the Holy Spirit, the plain fact is that it does not devote so much space to the doctrine that sets forth the truth about the Holy Spirit Himself as it does to certain other doctrines.

So we, in this little series of talks, have already said a good deal about the *work* of the Holy Spirit— at least *one* work of the Holy Spirit—when we spoke of the inspiration of the Bible, and if we do not say more about the Holy Spirit Himself that may perhaps be partially excused by the fact that the doctrine of the Holy Spirit, important though it is, could be set forth more briefly than, for example, the doctrine of the Son.

The teaching of the Bible about the Holy Spirit is found not only in the New Testament, but also in the Old Testament. The second verse of the Bible speaks of the Spirit of God as active at the beginning. "The Spirit of God," that verse says, "moved upon the face of the waters." We think also, of course, of the work of the Spirit in empowering the prophets when they came forward with a message from God. In some places the Spirit appears as the giver of some special qualification; but the Spirit also appears as determining a holy life.

"Take not thy holy spirit from me," says the Psalmist.[1] There is a tendency in some quarters to underestimate the richness of the Old Testament teaching regarding the Spirit of God.

But it must be admitted that in the Old Testament we have no clear presentation of the personal distinctness of the Spirit of God. We may have intimations of it, as we have intimations of the doctrine of the Trinity; but for clear teaching regarding it we must turn to the New Testament books.

In the New Testament books that clear teaching is certainly present. At first sight, indeed, it might not seem to be so abundant as we might expect it to be. The deity of the Holy Spirit is everywhere perfectly plain, but the distinct personality of the Holy Spirit does not seem to lie so clearly on the surface. Hence it is not surprising that in discussions of the doctrine of the Holy Spirit the question that is chiefly discussed is different from the question that is discussed with regard to Christ.

With regard to Christ, the distinct personality of the One who is presented is everywhere perfectly clear, and therefore argument is quite unnecessary about that. The question that needs discussion about Christ is the deity of the One spoken of. Christ appears to a superficial observer not as God but as a man. What needs to be done, therefore, is to show that superficial ob-

[1] Ps. 51:11.

server that this man, Jesus Christ, is both God and man.

But with regard to the Holy Spirit it is just the other way around. The deity of the Holy Spirit is everywhere perfectly clear; but what seems at first sight paradoxical, what seems to require discussion, is the true personality of the Spirit. It is clear without any discussion that the Spirit of God is God; but it might seem at first sight very strange that the Spirit of God should be a distinct person within the Godhead.

However—strange though that *is*—the Bible makes perfectly clear that it is true. A careful reading of the Bible shows that the true personality of the Holy Spirit, though not often made the subject of direct exposition, really underlies and gives meaning to everything that the Bible says about the Spirit of God.

For one thing, the great Trinitarian passages in the Bible really imply the personality of the Spirit. When, for example, our Lord in the "Great Commission" at the end of the Gospel according to Matthew commands the Apostles to make disciples of all the nations, "baptizing them in the name of the Father, and of the Son, and of the Holy Ghost," can He possibly mean that although the Father and the Son are persons, the Holy Ghost is a mere impersonal aspect of the being of the Father or of the Son? The perfect coördination of the three—Father, Son and Holy Ghost—would seem to make such an interpretation extremely unnatural. So it is also with the "Apostolic Benediction" at the end of the Second Epistle to the Corinthians: "The grace of the Lord Jesus Christ, and the love of God, and the communion of the Holy Ghost, be with you all." Here also to deny the distinct personality of the Spirit would seem almost to involve denying the distinct personality of the other two members of Paul's triad; and since that would of course be out of accord with the Apostle's whole teaching, it seems perfectly clear that he regards the Holy Ghost as a person just as he regards each of the other two.

But the passage where the personality of the Holy Spirit is most clearly and gloriously set forth is found in the intimate discourses of our Lord with His apostles, as those discourses are recorded in the Gospel according to John. Here our Lord speaks of the Holy Spirit as "another Comforter," or rather (by what is probably a better translation of the word) "another Advocate." The Holy Spirit, then, is in one sense "another" as over against Jesus; indeed in John 16:7 Jesus says that His, Jesus', departure means the Spirit's coming. "It is expedient for you that I go away: for if I go not away, the Comforter will not come unto you; but if I depart, I will send him unto you." It would hardly be possible to set forth more clearly than is done in these words the distinct personality of the Holy Spirit. He is not just an aspect of the person of Jesus; indeed, it is said that if Jesus departs He will come.

In another sense, indeed, even according to this very passage, the coming of the Spirit is the coming of Jesus; human analogies break down in the presence of the mystery of the Trinity. One cannot separate what the Son does and what the Father does from what the Spirit does as would be the case with three finite persons.

But, all the same, it remains true that the Holy Spirit does appear very clearly in this precious passage as a true person. He proceeds from the Father and the Son, but not as a mere emanation or a mere force but as a person who stands in a truly personal relationship with the two other persons in the Godhead. Again and again in this wonderful passage the personal relationship between all three persons of the Trinity is set forth. In one verse at least, our Lord uses the first person plural in speaking of Himself and God the Father. "If a man love me," He says, "he will keep my words: and my Father will love him, and we will come unto him, and make our abode with him." Here Jesus of Nazareth, a man who walked upon this earth, joins Himself with God the Father in a fellowship in which one person joins Himself with another. "*We* will come," He says. The human mind is aghast in the presence of that stupendous "we." God has certainly revealed to us wondrous things in His holy Word.

In this personal fellowship between the Father and the Son, the Holy Spirit, who is to be sent as another Comforter, appears as a third member of the fellowship. He stands in personal relation both to the Father and to the Son. "And I will pray the Father," says Jesus, "and he shall give you another Comforter, that he may abide with you for ever." Here the Spirit appears as being sent by the Father at the instance of the Son. In another place He appears as being sent by the Son, and yet as proceeding from the Father. "But when the Comforter is come, whom I will send unto you from the Father, even the Spirit of truth, which proceedeth from the Father, he shall testify of me." All through this passage the relationship between all three appears as a warm relationship of love between persons.

In the light of what our Lord here says, all thought of regarding the Father, Son and Holy Ghost as being merely three modes in which one Person works, or merely three aspects in which one Person may be regarded, is seen to be contrary to the very heart of what the Bible teaches. No, the Bible teaches us certainly that there are three persons in the Godhead.

But, in teaching us that, the Bible never allows us to forget the primary truth that there is but one God. That truth is pressed home in the Old Testament, but it is pressed home just as insistently in the New. When the New Testament teaches that Father, Son and Holy Ghost are three persons, it teaches with equal insistence that these three persons are one God. The New Testament writers never seem to be conscious that one of these two great truths could by any chance be regarded as in contradiction with the other. They are never for one moment conscious of any danger lest when they present the deity and the personality of the Son and of the Spirit they may lead men away from the unity of God. So in the Gospel of John Jesus says, "I and the Father are one";[2] yet in that same Gospel He says, about the Father and Himself, "*We* will come"; and in that same Gospel He says, "I will pray the Father, and he shall give you another Comforter." One God, three persons, each person God—so the Bible presents, in majestic harmony, what God has graciously revealed to us of the mysteries of His being.

The three persons of the Godhead are, as our Shorter Catechism puts it, "the same in substance, equal in power and glory." But is that so? Are the three persons of the Godhead really the same in substance and equal in power and glory?

One of the early heresies said, No. The Son is of like substance with the Father, said the adherents of that heresy, but not of the same substance. But widely removed indeed was that heresy from the teaching of the Bible. I know the difference between these two expressions—"of the same substance" and "of like substance" —has often been ridiculed as being the difference merely of an iota, the smallest letter in the Greek alphabet. The Greek word for "of like substance" has an iota in it, and the Greek word for "of the same sub-

[2] John 10:30.

stance" is that word with the iota left out. What a hair-splitting distinction, then, it is said, was that distinction which kept the Church in a turmoil for so many years! The whole trouble was over one tiny little "iota"!

Well, my friends, the unbelief of our day uses a great many arguments, but I doubt whether any argument ever was used in any debate that was much more foolish than this.

Is the difference between the meanings of words really to be measured by the number or the size of the letters wherein the words differ? In that case the difference between "just" and "unjust" for example, would be very slight. Just put the little syllable "un" in front of "just," and you get "unjust." What a very slight difference that is! So I suppose you are not at all interested in the question whether a man says your decisions are "just" or whether he says they are "unjust"! It is merely a difference of that little syllable! Even the word "not" is not a very big word. So I suppose it makes no difference to you whether somebody says you are a liar or whether he says you are not a liar! Why indulge in hair-splitting distinctions? Why quarrel over such a little word as "not"?

Well, we do quarrel over such little words and little letters. Little words and little letters sometimes make a vast deal of difference. So that little Greek letter, iota, made a whole world of difference in the great debate to which we have just referred. If Christ is said to be only of like substance with the Father, in the sense in which that early heresy meant it, then we have a miserable mythology that breaks down the gulf between the creature and the Creator, between the finite and the infinite. The Bible does no such thing. There is no such thing as "almost God" according to the Bible. The next thing less than the infinite, according to the Bible, is infinitely less.

So the Bible certainly teaches that the Son is of the same substance with the Father, and that He is equal to the Father in power and glory. Only so can He be very God. And it teaches that also with regard to the Holy Spirit. The three persons of the Godhead are, according to the Bible, the same in substance and equal in power and glory.

Do you know that triune God as your God, my friends? We pray that you may know Him so. We pray that the Holy Spirit may enable you to believe in the Son, and that, redeemed by His precious blood, you may stand in the Father's presence for evermore.

INDEX

INDEX

I. NAMES AND SUBJECTS

Abraham, 29.

Alps, the, 17.

America, 9; attack upon liberty in, 4.

American Academy of Political and Social Science, 12.

Amos, 53.

Annals, The, of American Academy of Political and Social Science, 12.

Anthropomorphism, 124.

Apologetics: necessity of, 61-67; various uses of, 63-67.

Apostles, the: supernatural revelation through, 30f.; supernatural authority of, 71; gave the New Testament books to the Church, 71; original, 229.

Apostles' Creed, the, 234f.

Apostolic Benediction, the, 129, 237f.

Appearances of the risen Christ: vision hypothesis regarding, 204-208; place of, 207-209; bodily nature of, 207f.; Galilean hypothesis regarding the place of, 213f.

Argument, necessity of, 61-67.

Aristotle, 91f.

Armistice, the, 3, 9.

Astronomy, 121.

Augustine, 124.

Authorized Version, the, 37, 42-44.

Autographs of the Biblical books, 39.

Bankers, international, 9.

Barnabas, 220.

Beatitudes, the, 162-164.

Beauty of nature, reveals God, 17-19.

Belgium, 3.

Belief, importance of, 97-102.

Bible, the: Christian view of, 2; is opposed to the making of religion a mere means to a higher end, 8; blessed work of, 12; approves the revelation of God through nature, 20f., and through conscience, 24f.; contains all the record of supernatural revelation that we can be certain about, 29-33; symmetry and completeness of the supernatural revelation recorded in, 29-31; inspiration and authority of, 32-86; is the Word of God, 32-44; inspiration of, 33-72; original languages of, 38; plainness of, 43f.; is a supernatural revelation as a whole, 44; writers of, used ordinary sources of information, 48f., 50-52, were

II. BIBLICAL PASSAGES

OLD TESTAMENT

NEW TESTAMENT

258 _Index_